The Complete Guide to
LANDSCAPE PROJECTS

Natural Landscape Design • Eco-friendly Water Features • Hardscaping • Landscape Plantings

Creative Publishing international

MINNEAPOLIS, MINNESOTA
www.creativepub.com

Creative Publishing international

Copyright © 2010
Creative Publishing international, Inc.
400 First Avenue North, Suite 300
Minneapolis, Minnesota 55401
1-800-328-0590
www.creativepub.com

Printed in China

10 9 8 7 6 5 4 3 2 1

Library of Congress Cataloging-in-Publication Data

The complete guide to landscape projects.
    p. cm.
  At head of title: Black & Decker.
  Includes index.
  ISBN-13: 978-1-58923-564-9 (soft cover)
  ISBN-10: 1-58923-564-9 (soft cover)
1. Landscape construction. I. Black & Decker Corporation (Towson, Md.) II. Title.

  TH4961.C6542 2010
  712--dc22

2010030580

President/CEO: Ken Fund

Home Improvement Group

Publisher: Bryan Trandem
Managing Editor: Tracy Stanley
Senior Editor: Mark Johanson

Creative Director: Michele Lanci-Altomare
Art Direction/Design: Jon Simpson, Brad Springer, James Kegley

Lead Photographer: Joel Schnell
Set Builder: James Parmeter
Production Managers: Laura Hokkanen, Linda Halls

Edition Editor: Kristen Hampshire
Page Layout Artist: Danielle Smith
Copy Editor: Chris Marshall
Shop Help: Charles Boldt

The Complete Guide to Landscape Projects
Created by: The Editors of Creative Publishing international, Inc., in cooperation with Black & Decker.
Black & Decker® is a trademark of The Black & Decker Corporation and is used under license.

NOTICE TO READERS

For safety, use caution, care, and good judgment when following the procedures described in this book. The publisher and Black & Decker cannot assume responsibility for any damage to property or injury to persons as a result of misuse of the information provided.

   The techniques shown in this book are general techniques for various applications. In some instances, additional techniques not shown in this book may be required. Always follow manufacturers' instructions included with products, since deviating from the directions may void warranties. The projects in this book vary widely as to skill levels required: some may not be appropriate for all do-it-yourselfers, and some may require professional help.

   Consult your local building department for information on building permits, codes, and other laws as they apply to your project.

Contents

The Complete Guide to
Landscape Projects

Contents (Cont.)

Introduction

We're spending more time at home these days, investing in our properties to convert our outdoor spaces from basic back yards into elaborate living rooms with areas for dining, lounging, gardening, playing, and perhaps even swimming. Rather than planning vacations, many of us are plotting our next, big outdoor adventure—and we're talking about landscape projects. There's great satisfaction that can be gained from completing a pond, building an arbor, laying a flagstone pathway, or planting a colorful landscape bed. And we're recognizing that the more of this we do ourselves, the larger our budget is to do even more!

The Complete Guide to Landscape Projects will teach you how to create an outdoor living space with features both luxurious and practical. We'll walk you through the process from beginning to end, starting with providing detailed tools and materials lists for each project. We give you tutorials for basic building techniques, and inspiration for interesting finishes and treatments that will customize projects to suit the character of your property and your personal preferences. For instance, our outdoor fireplace project shows you how to finish the exterior in stone, brick, or stucco. We give you options, and we outline careful guidelines along the way. Think of this book as your instructor as you take on important projects that will enhance your yard.

Whether you're creating a landscape from scratch or renovating a mature property, we have ideas for you. And better yet, each project provides step-by-step instructions with color photography. We think showing you how projects come together is just as important as telling you with our field-tested directions.

There are projects in this book suitable for big back yards, quaint courtyards, small gardens, city landscapes, suburban yards, and country estates. You can depend on this book for a variety of do-able landscape projects that will stand the test of time.

Now, let's get started! It's time to get your hands dirty and begin building the landscape of your dreams. Who needs a vacation when you can escape every day in your own back yard?

Lawncare & Design

A successful landscaping project requires a firm foundation. Essentially, this comes down to dirt and turf. Regardless of what you are building, your yard must have good drainage and healthy soil. This may require that you re-grade your yard, improve drainage, create water runoff paths, or build retaining walls or other landscape features to create level areas and control erosion. In addition to its visual appeal, the turf in your yard plays an important role in the infrastructure by retaining topsoil and preventing erosion. Promoting turf health through proper mowing practices, adequate watering, lawn nutrition, and regular maintenance will help preserve your landscape for years to come.

In this chapter:

- Lawncare Basics
- Landscape Materials
- Tools
- Landscape Design

Lawncare Basics

Regular lawn maintenance is an important element of a successful landscape, but it does require dedication. Keeping up with duties such as mowing, watering, and turf nutrition will prevent disease and keep weeds from forming—and you'll use fewer control products if you simply mow and water regularly and sensibly. Addressing and correcting occasional problems is another requirement of homeownership.

As we pay closer attention to the chemicals we pour on to our lawns and the way we manage lawn problems in an effort to be more mindful of the world around us—you hear about this as "going green" or being "sustainable"—these lawn basics (cultural practices) become even more essential. By following some core cultural practices, you can reach the goal of a lush, healthy lawn without all the additives.

Controlling weeds keeps turf grass healthy so it can perform to its fullest as a canvas for landscaping creativity. Most yards will benefit from a multi-pronged approach of pulling weeds, selective chemical spraying, and organic weed control measures.

Regular lawnmowing is an important part of any lawn and yard maintenance program. A cordless lawnmower is a clean, quiet equipment option.

Lawnmowing Rules of Thumb

Proper lawnmowing practices will promote turf growth, discourage weeds and disease, and protect soil from losing moisture. That's why you don't want to give your lawn a buzz cut, even if that means you can avoid mowing more than once a week during growing season. Always aim to cut off the top third of turf in a single pass. The recommended height for your lawn depends on turfgrass variety, so check with your local university extension for specific recommendations. The more you know about your turf, the better you can manage its growth in a healthy way.

As for timing, while Saturday morning might be when you your schedule allows for some outdoor leisure, your lawn won't appreciate a mow that morning if it rained all night and the ground is sopping wet. For safety and turf health reasons, don't mow when grass is wet. Mower wheels mat down turf, and those stressed areas prevent sunlight from reaching roots—besides, diseases like those dark places.

As you mow your lawn, you'll realize just how many imperfections may exist. Most lawns aren't perfect squares, smooth and flat. You'll likely deal with ruts, slopes, and curvy bed lines. Handle all areas with care, and take these safety precautions when mowing:

- Use a trimmer in tight areas where an angle could compromise your safety; or use a walk-behind mower rather than a riding lawn tractor.
- Use a line trimmer around trees before mowing.
- Mow across slopes when using zero-turn riding mowers and walk-behind mowers. Mow directly up and down slopes when operating a riding mower.
- Avoid sudden stops or turns when mowing slopes, and always mow slowly and look behind you when operating in reverse.
- Always clear the mowing area of debris and children's toys before mowing. Be sure children and pets are clear of the yard before mowing.

Mowing on Slopes

Mow directly up and down slopes when operating a standard (not zero-turn radius) riding lawn mower.

Mow across slopes when cutting grass with a walk-behind mower.

Watering Basics

The amount of water your turf requires depends on many factors, including the grass variety in your lawn and the soil conditions. Check with your local university extension or lawn care specialist for information on exactly how much water your lawn requires to stay healthy. That way, you won't deprive it—or over-water it and waste natural resources.

Soil plays a major role in turf health. The type of soil directly beneath the turf determines the rate at which water soaks in or is directed away as runoff.

Essentially, soil is a filter that water must pass through to reach grass roots. So if soil is sandy and porous, water reaches roots quickly—sometimes so quickly that roots don't have a chance to soak the water up before it falls through the soil profile. Sandy soils require deep watering.

Clay soils do not absorb moisture well. If you notice puddles of water forming on the ground after you water, it is likely that you have clay soil. Clay does retain moisture longer than porous soil, but the trick to watering turf in clay soil is getting enough water down to the roots of the grass. Often, puddled water simply runs off without penetrating deeper into the soil. Water clay soils more frequently for shorter periods of time.

Your soil might be a combination of clay and sand, or a silt composition that readily accepts water. The best advice is to carefully observe how your yard reacts to watering, and know how much water your grass type needs in the first place.

Avoid over-watering your lawn by purchasing a rain gauge to find out how much water grass receives each week. When you do sprinkle, it is best to do so in the morning while temperatures are still relatively cool and the water won't evaporate as quickly. Night watering can promote fungus and other disease because moisture will sit on grass blades for hours. Overly moist soil prevents oxygen from reaching grass roots and can result in root rot.

The Right Height ▶

How low should you mow? The primary rule is to cut off one-third of the turf plant at one time. Whether you have just returned from vacation to find turf gone wild or you mow religiously every few days, the same rule applies. Your goal is to maintain the recommended height for your lawn and avoid giving your turf a crew cut.

The recommended height for your lawn varies with turfgrass variety. Most grasses thrive when cut at 2 to 3 inches in the fall and spring. Set your cutting deck higher in the summer, so grass can soak in the sun, allowing it to grow and develop. Always mind the recommended cutting height for your turfgrass variety. For example, if you live in Florida and your lawn is St. Augustine grass, turf height should range from 2½ to 4 inches. Following the one-third rule, if your lawn is 7 inches tall, you should remove a little more than 2 inches at one time.

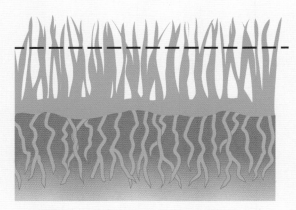

By mowing at the proper height and controlling thatch, water will soak in more efficiently and better quench roots' thirst. You'll use less water and get better results.

The Trickle-Down Effect ▶

Sandy soils are more porous and allow water to seep through quickly. Clay soils retain water for longer periods of time, but the moisture takes longer to absorb.

Clay soil   Sandy soil

Feeding the Lawn

Fertilizer is essentially a vitamin boost for your turf. It is most important if you are growing grass in challenging conditions—as many of us are. The key is to strike a happy balance when using lawn care products by applying the proper amounts at the optimum times. In addition to chemical fertilizers, there are organic methods of feeding the lawn, such as top-dressing with compost products following an aeration. Also, regular maintenance tasks, such as mowing and watering, keep your lawn healthy so the need for amendments is minimized. If you prefer, you can follow an organic lawn regimen. You'll find many lawn care companies dedicated to "green" lawn care using a minimal amount of product to achieve a healthy lawn. But keep in mind your vision for the grass: You're not likely to achieve a golf-course green lawn with an organic program. But then, you also won't be using the amount of product that stoking grass into super-green mode requires.

Here are some basics you'll want to build into your plant turf nutrition program:

- Slow-release fertilizer feeds plants gradually over a period of time.
- Herbicides are weed-control products available in several forms: selective, nonselective, contact, and systemic. Selective herbicides knock down certain weed species without affecting the growth of other plants. Most herbicides are selective.

Nonselective herbicides wipe out all green plants. You might use these when clearing a grassy spot to build a pond or plant bed. Contact herbicides are spot treatments, and these generally require repeat applications. If you prefer not to apply product to your entire lawn, you'd use contact herbicides to manage weeds that crop up in specific areas.
- Pesticides and insecticides target lawn care problems and are generally reserved for use by professionals, who can accurately identify disease and insect problems and prepare a treatment plan.

Organic soil builders, including composted manure, peat moss, and bone meal, improve soil in the same way as chemical additives but pose less danger to the environment from rainwater runoff.

Using a Drop Spreader

Always check that the spreader's release door is closed before filling the hopper with product. Set the spreader over a paved surface so you can easily sweep up spills.

When operating a drop spreader, always overlap passes. Line up the center of the spreader to the center of your last wheel track.

The best way to apply granular fertilizer accurately is to divide the application in half. Apply the first half in one direction, then apply the second half in a path perpendicular to your first pass.

Landscape Materials

From natural to manmade, the range of materials available today for landscape projects offers many options. You may choose materials that blend with your exiting yard and architectural features, or you may go another direction entirely, such as preferring a brand-new element to your yard because it is long-lasting or "green."

Wood remains the single most popular building material for outdoor construction, but stonescaping projects have grown in popularity with a host of natural and cultured products that are durable and affordable.

Pressure-treated lumber stamps list the type of preservative and the chemical retention level, as well as the exposure rating and the name and location of the treating company.

Cedar grade stamps list the mill number, moisture content, species, lumber grade, and membership association. Western red cedar (WRC) or incense cedar (INC) for decks should be heartwood (HEART) with a maximum moisture content of 15% (MC15).

Cedar

Pressure-treated pine

Redwood

Pine

Cedar lattice

Bark mulch

METALS

Metal of various types is often used for fences and gates. Aluminum offers a sturdy, lightweight, and waterproof material that is available in a variety of designs. Aluminum is also a popular material for lamp posts. Galvanized chain-link steel is also a popular choice for fencing, because it is relatively maintenance free and reasonably priced. Chain link is also a good choice where security is a concern. Traditional wrought iron, though more expensive, is used for fencing, railings, gates, and patio furniture.

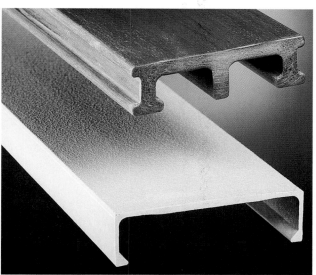

PLASTICS

Plastic materials such as PVC vinyl and fiberglass reinforced plastic (FRP) are generally used in applications such as fencing, arbors, deck skirting, and lawn edging. Many styles and sizes are available, and they are strong, versatile, and require no maintenance. Some fence materials are sold as kits, making installation easy.

COMPOSITE MATERIALS

Composite materials blend together wood fibers and plastics to create a rigid product that will not rot, splinter, warp, or crack. These boards can be cut with a circular saw, require little to no maintenance, and don't need to be painted or stained. Although they're typically more expensive than wood and other alternatives, composites are extremely durable and over the life of a structure can be less expensive than wood, which may need to be replaced. Composites are a good choice for decking, railing systems, and landscaping timbers.

MANUFACTURED STONE

Manufactured stone is designed to resemble natural stone, but because it's more uniform it is easier to install and generally costs less. Brick, concrete, and glass block are being offered in more styles all the time, giving you a lot of flexibility to build distinctive projects that are also reasonably priced. Decorative concrete block can be used to make screen walls and is available in many colors.

Concrete paver slabs, available in several shapes and sizes, are used for laying simple walkways and patios. They're available in a standard finish, a smooth aggregate finish, or can be colored and molded to resemble brick. Concrete paver slabs are relatively inexpensive and quite easy to work with. They're usually laid in a bed of sand and require no mortar. Their surface is generally finished so the smooth gravel aggregate is exposed, but they are also available in plain pavers and aggregate.

Paver bricks resemble traditional kiln-dried clay bricks but are more durable and easier to install. Paver bricks come in many colors and shapes and are ideal for paving patios, walkways, and driveways. Many varieties are available in interlocking shapes that can be combined with standard bricks to create decorative patterns, such as herringbone and basket weave. Edging blocks are precast in different sizes for creating boundaries to planting areas, lawns, loose-fill paths, and retaining walls.

Interlocking retaining wall blocks

Molded paver slabs

Paver bricks

Exposed aggregate paver slabs

Concrete paver slabs

Bricks, concrete blocks, and glass blocks are best suited for projects where the masonry units are mortared together. They should not be used interchangeably with pavers and other products that are designed to be loose-stacked and sand-set.

NATURAL STONE

Natural stone offers beautiful color, interesting texture, and great durability, making it one of the very best building materials for outdoor construction. Although it is more expensive than many other materials, if it fits in your budget, you're not likely to regret choosing stone. It is a good choice for edging, walls, walkways, ponds, fountains, and waterfalls. Natural stone is also used to accent flowers and plants creating depth in garden areas (this is a great way to use stone if you can't afford huge amounts of it).

Each type of stone offers a distinctive look, as well as a specific durability and workability. The nature of your project will often dictate the best form of stone to use. When shopping for stone, describe your project to the supplier and ask him or her to suggest a stone that meets your needs.

Fieldstone, sometimes called river rock, is used to build retaining walls, ornamental garden walls, and rock gardens. When split into smaller pieces, fieldstone can be used in projects with mortar. When cut into small pieces, or quarried stone, fieldstone is called cobblestone, a common material in walks and paths.

Ashlar, or wall stone, is quarried granite, marble, or limestone that has been smooth-cut into large blocks, ideal for creating clean lines with thin mortar joints. Cut stone works well for stone garden walls, but because of its expense, its use is sometimes limited to decorative wall caps.

Flagstone is large slabs of sedimentary rock with naturally flat surfaces. Limestone, sandstone, slate, and shale are the most common types of flagstone. It is usually cut into pieces up to 3 inches thick, for use in walks, steps, and patios. Smaller pieces—less than 16 inches square—are often called steppers.

Veneer stone is natural or manufactured stone cut or molded for use in nonload-bearing, cosmetic applications, such as facing exterior walls or freestanding concrete block walls.

Rubble is irregular pieces of quarried stone, usually with one split or finished face. It is widely used in wall construction.

Fieldstone is stone gathered from fields, dry riverbeds, and hillsides. It is used in wall construction.

Flagstone consists of large slabs of quarried stone cut into pieces up to 3" thick. It is used in walks, steps, and patios.

A stone yard is a great place to get ideas and see the types of stone that are available. This stone yard includes a display area that identifies different types of stone and suggests ways they can be used.

Concrete

Poured concrete is used for driveways, walkways, and patios because of its exceptional strength. Although it is sometimes criticized for its bland appearance, concrete in modern use is often tinted or given a surface finish that lets it simulate brick pavers or flagstone at a fraction of the cost. Concrete can also be formed into curves and other shapes, such as landscape ponds or fountains.

Another option for large projects, such as a driveway or patio slab, is to have premixed concrete delivered by a ready-mix supplier. If you choose this method, make sure you have plenty of help on hand to move and finish the concrete quickly.

Bagged concrete mix comes in many formulations. The selection you're likely to encounter varies by region and by time of year, but the basic products most home centers stock include: all-purpose concrete (A, C) for posts, footings, and slabs; sand mix (B) for topping and casting; Portland cement (D) for mixing with aggregate, sand, and water to make your own concrete; high/early concrete (E) for driveways and other projects that demand greater shock and crack resistance; fast-setting concrete (F) for setting posts and making repairs; specialty blends for specific purposes, such as countertop mix (G), which comes premixed with polyester fibers and additives that make it suitable for countertops.

Liquid concrete products can be added to the concrete mix while blending or applied after the concrete sets up. Concrete sealer (A) is applied to concrete immediately after set-up to seal and to assist with the curing. Bonding additive (B), usually latex or acrylic based, is added to the dry mix instead of water (or in addition to water) to make the concrete more elastic and help new concrete bond to old concrete by sliding into crevices in old concrete surfaces. Concrete colorant (C) is added to the concrete while liquid for even coloring that goes all the way through the material. Dry pigments also may be added to the wet mixture, or they are sometimes scattered onto the surface of concrete slabs during the troweling stage. Stucco and mortar color (D) can be added to finish coat stucco, mason mix, surface-bonding cement, and heavy-duty masonry coating. It is often premixed with water.

Block & Mortar

Laying brick and block is a precise business. Many of the tools necessary for these projects relate to establishing and maintaining true, square, and level structures, while others relate to cutting the masonry units and placing the mortar. It makes sense to purchase tools you'll use again, but it's more cost effective to rent specialty items, such as a brick splitter.

Mortar mixes: Type N, a medium-strength mortar for above-grade outdoor use in nonload-bearing (freestanding) walls, barbeques, chimneys, and tuck-pointing (A); refractory mortar, a calcium aluminate mortar that is resistant to high temperatures, used for mortaring around firebrick in fireplaces and barbeques (B); Type S, a high-strength mortar for outdoor use at or below grade, typically used in foundations, retaining walls, driveways, walks, and patios (C); mortar tint for coloring mortar (D); and you'll need water for mixing mortar so a hose is needed (E) (a sprayer attachment is needed later to clean the surface).

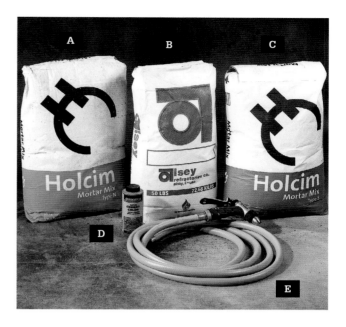

Common types of brick and block used for residential construction include: decorative block (A) available colored or plain; decorative concrete pavers (B); fire brick (C); standard 8 × 8 × 16" concrete block (D); half block (E); combination corner block (F); queen-sized brick (G); standard brick pavers (H); standard building bricks (I); and limestone wall cap (J).

Loose Materials

Loose materials for patios and walkways encompass a wide range of natural elements, from gravel to wood chips to small river stones. You can use a loose material by itself to create a simple patio or path surface or use it as infill between an arrangement of heavier materials, such as flagstone or large, concrete stepping pavers. In contrast to the solidity and permanence of traditional paving, loose materials have a casual, summery feel. Walking over a pathway of crushed stone or wood chips can feel like a stroll down a country lane or a walk through the woods.

As a primary surface, loose materials offer several practical advantages. They drain well, are forgiving of uneven ground, and can be replenished and graded with a rake for a quick facelift. They also tend to be much less expensive than most other paving options and couldn't be easier to install. In a typical installation, start with a bed of compacted gravel and cover it with landscape fabric to inhibit weed growth and separate the gravel base from the surface material. Then, spread out the surface material a few inches thick, compact it if necessary, and you're done! For simpler applications, such as a lightly traveled garden path, you can often skip the gravel base and lay the landscape fabric right over leveled and tamped soil. In most cases, it's best to include a raised edging of some kind to contain the materials and maintain the shape of the paved surface.

Selecting Loose Materials

Because different loose materials can have very different textures and properties, it's important to choose the right surface for the application. Here's a look at some of the most popular materials for patios and walkways:

Decomposed granite: A popular choice for level patios, paths, and driveways, decomposed granite (DG) can be compacted to a relatively smooth, flat, hard surface. DG consists of small pieces of granite ranging in size from sand-size grains to a quarter inch—this size variation is the reason this material is so compactable. DG is available in various natural shades of gray, brown, and tan. Due to its gritty, sandy finish that can stick to your shoes, DG is not a good choice for surfaces that receive heavy traffic directly to and from the house.

Pea gravel and crushed stone: Pea gravel and crushed stone include a broad range of gravel, from fairly fine textures to very coarse. Pea gravel is small- to medium-sized stone that is either mechanically crushed or shaped naturally by water. Crushed stone typically consists of coarse, jagged pieces in various sizes, generally larger than pea gravel. Many types of gravel are compactable, but usually less so than DG.

Loose materials can work well on their own or as a complement to surrounding elements. In this landscape, buff-colored gravel serves as both a primary surface and an infill material for a stepping stone path. The natural look of the gravel provides a nice contrast to the formal paver walkway and patio.

Gravel made up of round stones is more comfortable to walk on than jagged materials.

River rock: Smoothed and rounded by water or machines, river rock ranges from small stones to baseball-sized (and larger) rocks. These smooth surfaces make it more comfortable to walk on than jagged gravel but it is also less compactable and easily displaced underfoot. Larger stones are difficult to walk on and are more suitable for infill and accent areas than for primary paving surfaces.

Wood chips: Wood chips and mulch are commonly used as groundcover in planting beds, gardens, and flowerbeds. Most types are soft and springy underfoot, and many can be used for light-traffic paths and even children's play areas. Wood chips come in a wide variety of grades, colors, and textures. In general, finely chopped and consistent materials are more expensive and more formal in appearance than coarse blends. The term mulch is often used interchangeably with wood chips but can also describe roughly chopped wood and other organic matter that's best suited for beds and ground cover. Most loose material made of wood needs some replenishing every two to four years.

Both stone and wood loose materials are typically sold in bulk at landscape and garden centers and by the bag at home centers. Buying in bulk is often much less expensive for all but the smallest jobs. Landscape and garden suppliers typically offer bulk deliveries for a reasonable flat fee. Due to the variance in terminology and appearance of loose materials, be sure to visit the supplier and take a look at the materials you're buying firsthand, so you know exactly what to expect.

Pea gravel

Crushed stone

River rock

Decomposed granite

Wood chips

Estimating & Ordering Materials

Even with small projects, it's important to take careful measurements and estimate accurately. Landscaping materials are bulky and are expensive and time consuming to transport, so accurate estimating will save you time and money.

Begin compiling a materials list by reviewing the scale drawing of your building plans (pages 30 to 33), then use the information here to estimate materials. Once you have developed a materials list, add 10 percent to the estimate for each item to allow for waste and small oversights.

The cost of your project will depend upon which building materials you choose. You can save money by choosing materials that are readily available in your area. This is particularly true of natural stone products. Choosing stone that is quarried locally is far less expensive than exotic stone transported long distances. Lumber, metal, and plastics can also vary widely in price, depending on where they're milled or manufactured.

Most of what you need is available at large, general-purpose home centers, but for landscaping projects you may want to buy some materials from specialty retailers. A large concrete project, for example, will be cheaper if you buy ready-mix concrete instead of bagged concrete mix from your home center.

If you plan on working with specialty or alternative materials, such as vinyl fencing or composite decking, many home centers will have a select range of styles and sizes on hand but can also order specialty materials for you.

A contractor's calculator can convert measurements and estimate concrete volume. The calculator isn't very expensive and will relieve you of complex math conversions. It's also handy for estimating fencing materials and paint coverage.

HOW TO ESTIMATE MATERIALS

Sand, gravel, topsoil (2" layer)	surface area (sq. ft.) ÷ 100 = tons needed
Standard brick pavers for walks (2" layer)	surface area (sq. ft.) × 5 = number of pavers needed
Standard bricks for walls and pillars (4 × 8")	surface area (sq. ft.) × 7 = number of bricks needed (single-brick thickness)
Poured concrete (4" layer)	surface area (sq. ft.) × .012 = cubic yards needed
Flagstone	surface area (sq. ft.) ÷ 100 = tons needed
Interlocking block (2" layer)	area of wall face (sq. ft.) × 1.5 = number of blocks needed
Ashlar stone for 1-ft.-thick walls	area of wall face (sq. ft.) ÷ 15 = tons of stone needed
Rubble stone for 1-ft.-thick walls	area of wall face (sq. ft.) ÷ 35 = tons of stone needed
8 × 8 × 16" concrete block for freestanding walls	height of wall (ft.) × length of wall (ft.) × 1.125 = number of blocks needed

AMOUNT OF CONCRETE NEEDED (CU. FT.)

Number of 8"-diameter footings	Depth of footings (ft.)			
	1	2	3	4
2	¾	1½	2¼	3
3	1	2¼	3½	4½
4	1½	3	4½	6
5	2	3¾	5¾	7½

DRY INGREDIENTS FOR SELF-MIX

Amount of concrete needed (cu. ft.)	94-lb. bags of portland cement	Cubic feet of sand	Cubic feet of gravel	60-lb. bags of premixed dry concrete
1	⅙	⅓	½	2
2	⅓	⅔	1	4
3	½	1½	3	6
4	¾	1¾	3½	8
5	1	2¼	4½	10
10	2	4½	9	20

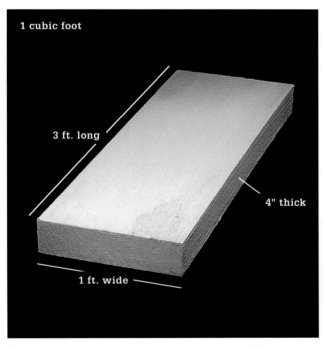

1 cubic foot

3 ft. long

4" thick

1 ft. wide

To estimate concrete volume, measure the width and length of the project in feet, then multiply the dimensions to get the square footage. Measure the thickness in feet (4" thick equals ⅓ ft.), then multiply the square footage times the thickness to get the cubic footage. For example, 1 ft. × 3 ft. × ⅓ ft. = 1 cu. ft. Twenty-seven cubic feet equals 1 cubic yard.

CONCRETE COVERAGE

Volume	Thickness	Surface coverage
1 cu. yd.	2"	160 sq. ft.
1 cu. yd.	3"	110 sq. ft.
1 cu. yd.	4"	80 sq. ft.
1 cu. yd.	5"	65 sq. ft.
1 cu. yd.	6"	55 sq. ft.
1 cu. yd.	8"	40 sq. ft.

Local brick and stone suppliers will often help you design your project and advise you about estimating materials, local building codes, and climate considerations.

Tools

The landscaper's tool shed contains a range of basic hand tools, larger specialty tools, masonry tools, and power tools. As you take on projects in this book, you'll gradually expand your everyday tool box to a well-rounded collection that could easily fill a shed. You may not want to purchase every tool, and that's where rental centers come in handy. Many landscape supply and hardware stores also have equipment available for rent. If you'll use the equipment one time, or on a very limited basis, this is the most cost-effective way to acquire the tools you need without investing heavily in equipment that will sit unused 99 percent of the time. Let's face it: While a front-end loader would be a fun outdoor toy, it's just not a necessity for most of us.

For tools you decide to purchase, invest in the best you can afford. Metal tools should be made from high-carbon steel with smoothly finished surfaces. Hand tools should be well-balanced and have tight, comfortably molded handles. Pick up the tool. How does it feel? Ergonomics are a big deal because you'll be spending lots of time handling your basic tools. Consider the length of the shaft on shovels, landscape rakes, etc. You can find adjustable options that allow you to "size" the equipment to suit your body.

Portable power tools that come in handy for landscape construction include: power miter saw (A), cordless drill/driver (B), reciprocating saw (cordless or corded) (C), hammer drill with ½" chuck for drilling masonry (D), jigsaw (E), nailer (cordless or pneumatic) (F), circular saw (cordless or corded) (G).

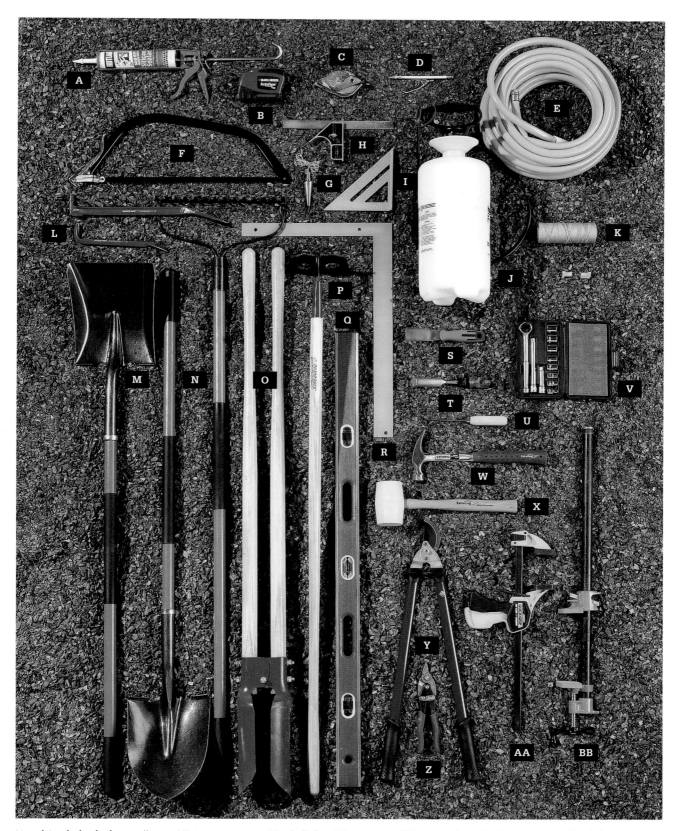

Hand tools include: caulk gun (A), tape measure (B), chalk line (C), compass (D), garden hose (E), bow saw (F), plumb bob (G), combination square (H), speed square (I), pressure sprayer (J), mason's line (K), square and round shovels (M), garden rake (N), posthole digger (O), hoe (P), carpenter's level (Q), framing square (R), putty knife (S), wood chisel (T), awl (U), socket wrench set (V), hammer (W), rubber mallet (X), pruning shears (Y), metal shears (Z), bar clamps (AA), and pipe clamps (BB).

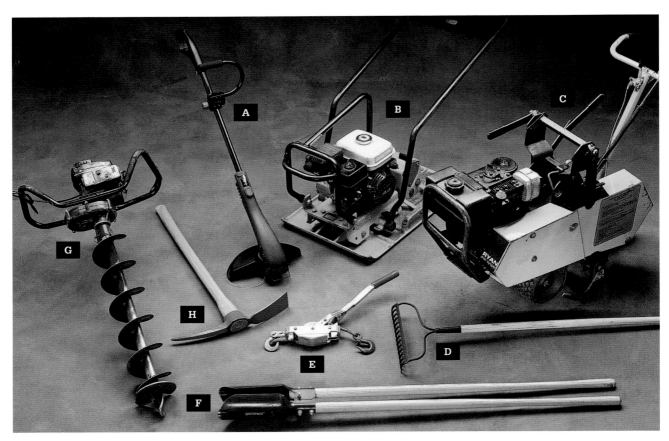

Specialty tools for landscape and yard work include: weed trimmer for clearing light brush (A), power tamper for compacting soil and subbase material (B), power sod cutter (C), garden rake or bow rake (D), come-along manual winch to assist in moving heavy objects (E), post-hole digger (F), gas-powered auger (G), pick axe (H).

A skid loader can be rented by the hour or by the day to help you with major earth-moving projects. Be sure to get plenty of detailed operating instructions from the rental center staff.

A wheelbarrow is an essential tool for practically any landscaping project. A 4-cubic foot, steel wheelbarrow like the one above is small enough that most DIYers can handle it. If you'll be moving larger amounts of soil, stone, or bricks, look for a larger 6-to-7 cubic foot model, preferably with poly or structural foam construction.

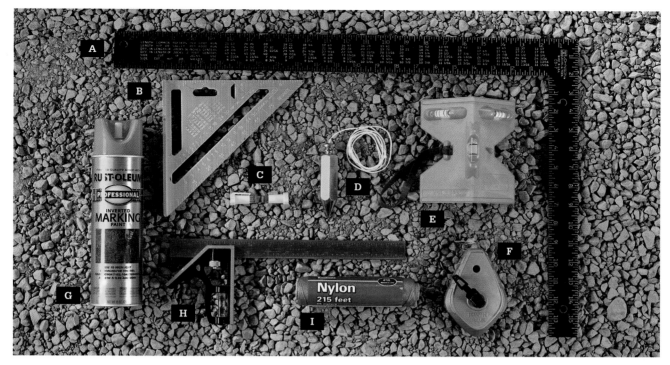

Layout, marking, and leveling tools: framing square (A), speed square (B), line level (C), plumb bob (D), post level (E), chalk line (F), landscape marking paint (G), combination square (H), mason's string (I).

Safety Gear ▸

Safety gear for stonework includes: protective knee pads (A), steel-toe work boots (B), hard hat (C), eye protection (D), hearing protection (E), particle mask (F), sturdy gloves (G).

Hardware & Fasteners

Although they're rarely visible, the metal brackets, screws, nails, bolts, and other hardware items can be crucial to a successful landscaping project.

Metal anchors are a common type of hardware used for landscape projects and decks. Some of the most common types are shown in the photo below. Used to reinforce framing connections, many of the anchors called for in the various projects (and all of the anchors in the sheds and outbuilding projects) are Simpson Strong-Tie brand, which are commonly available at lumberyards and home centers. If you can't find what you need on the shelves, look through the manufacturer's catalog, or visit their Web site (see page 235). Always use the fasteners recommended by the manufacturer.

The chemicals now used in pressure-treated lumber may require metal connectors specially designed to withstand the corrosive effect of these chemicals. Specifically, manufacturers suggest that metal connectors used with pressure-treated lumber be galvanized with a hot-dip process rather than a mechanical zinc plating. Triple-dipped, hot-dipped galvanized fasters are the best.

Alternatively, you can use stainless steel fasteners with pressure-treated lumber. Do not use aluminum fasteners with pressure-treated lumber.

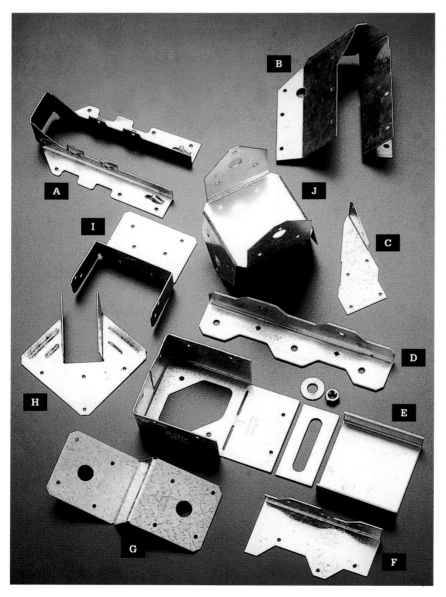

Metal connectors are time-savers when doing landscape construction. Buy triple-dipped, galvanized connectors when available. Types with possible application in landscape construction include: joist hanger (A), skewed joist hanger (B), rafter tie (C), stair cleat (D), 3-part post standoff with washer and nut (E), corner bracket (F), deck joist tie (G), hurricane tie (H), post cap/saddle (I), stand-off post anchors (J).

Nails, screws, bolts, washers, nuts, and lag screws for outdoor use must be resistant to corrosion. Generally, metals are coated with some additional material to make them weatherproof. You may see products coated with materials like epoxy and ceramic. But the best choice may be the old standby—galvanized steel.

Galvanized steel has a zinc coating. If you are working with pressure-treated lumber, it's important that the nails, screws, bolts, and other fasteners be double or triple hot-dipped, a process that improves and thickens the bond between the zinc and steel. Look for the phrase "hot-dipped" or "HDG" on the package when buying galvanized hardware.

Stainless steel is the other common alternative when working with pressure-treated lumber. Although these fasteners are somewhat expensive, they have excellent weather resistance.

When working with composite lumber, use the fasteners recommended by the lumber manufacturer. "Composite" screws often are designed with a special head shape that prevents the screws from mushrooming when driven into composite material.

There are a number of head-driving options available for exterior-rated screws. Square and torx-drive screws will not slip while fastening like phillips heads. Posi-drive screws are very popular because they combine phillips and square-drive heads, giving you a choice of which to use.

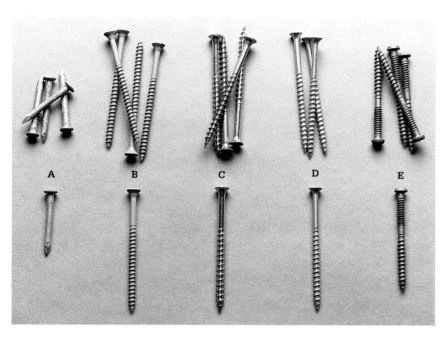

Specialty nails and screws for landscaping projects include: Metal connector nails (A), color-plated screws (B), stainless steel screws (C), galvanized screws (D), composite screws (E). Composite screws have a slightly different head and thread configuration.

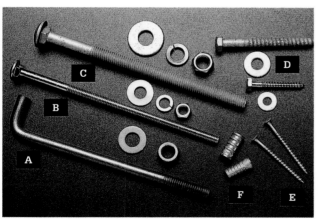

Common fasteners include: J-bolt with nut and washer (A), carriage bolts with washers and nuts (B, C), galvanized lag screws and washers (D), corrosion-resistant deck screws (E), masonry anchors (F).

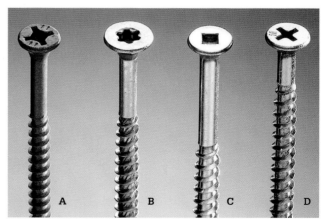

Head styles for exterior screws include: Posi-drive (A), torx (B), square drive (C), and phillips (D).

Landscape Design

Before you dig into the projects in this book, take the time to brainstorm and make a wish list of how you imagine your outdoor space could look. If your goal is to create an outdoor room, consider what elements you'll want to include to accomplish this. Now, get out a scratch pad and begin making some rough drawings of your dream landscape. Think big picture, not project-by-project. Each feature we'll teach you to build complements another project, and you'll find as you build that you want to keep adding more elements to your outdoor space. There's no limit! But, you'll want to take this grand plan in stages, which is why your first task is to create a priority list and start with defining, foundation elements: patios, fences, retaining walls.

Now that you have an idea of how various projects will fit into your overall landscape design, you'll want to focus on the task at hand. While not all landscape projects require a detailed plan, drawings will help you navigate complicated projects with many steps. Here, we'll show you how to survey your yard, draw a site map, sketch bubble plans, draw a landscape design, and create a working drawing you can take to the field—your back yard, that is.

Measuring your yard doesn't have to be done with precise surveying equipment, but it is very helpful to spend some time with a tape measure before you begin drawing plans. These measurements provide the information you need to create all other landscape drawings. Good measurements are also essential for projects where building permits are required.

Make a rough sketch of your yard, then make measurements that are as accurate as possible. Some landscape projects require digging, so contact your local utility companies to mark the locations of any underground power, gas, or communications lines. If the property boundaries aren't clear, you may also need to contact your county surveyor's office to come and mark the precise boundary lines for you. This can be very important if your landscaping plans will include a fence or garden wall that adjoins the property line.

Straight lines and square corners are easy enough to measure and mark, but it can be a bit harder to precisely locate features that have irregular shapes, or features that are angled in relation to the main property lines. In this case, you can use a method called triangulation to determine precise positions. On a square lot, for example, you can determine the location of a large tree most accurately by measuring the distance to the tree from two corners of the property.

On a yard with significant slopes, make cross-section drawings, called elevations, to indicate the vertical rise of the landscape. Elevations are drawings that show the landscape as viewed from the side. They'll be important for planning fence, garden wall, or retaining wall projects.

Measure the position of all the features of your yard, relative to the property lines. This work may require a helper and a long tape measure.

Use the survey measurements to create a rough drawing of your yard.

Using your survey measurements and the rough sketch, you'll now create a more accurate and precise drawing of your yard, called a site map. This is nothing more than a drawing that shows the basic permanent features of your yard. It will include the property lines and all buildings on the site, as well as other permanent structures, like driveways or large trees.

The site map is an overhead view of your yard, drawn to scale. It is the basis for the finished landscape design.

A scale of ⅛" = 1 ft. is a good scale to use for site maps and landscape plans. At this scale, you can map a yard as big as 60 × 80 ft. on a standard sheet of paper, or an 80 × 130-ft. yard on a 11 × 17" sheet of paper. If your yard is bigger than this, you can tape several sheets together.

Convert all the measurements you made in the survey to scale measurements. Then outline your yard by drawing the straight boundaries to scale.

Where you triangulated measurements from property corners, set a compass to the scale measurements, then draw arcs on the drawing. Where the arcs intersect is the precise location of the triangulated measurements.

Use a plastic triangle and ruler to mark the edges and corners of all structures within the boundaries of your yard.

Sketching Bubble Plans

Bubble plans are rough sketches in which you play with different ideas for arranging features within your overall yard. They are a great way to test out different ideas before committing to them. You might, for example, draw your yard with a patio positioned in different locations to see how it feels in relationship to your deck and garden beds.

Draw lots of variations of your ideas, and feel free to play with ideas that seem a little extreme. Professional designers sometimes go through dozens of ideas before settling on one that will eventually turn into a final landscape design.

The place to start is with lots of photocopies of the site map you've created. Or, you can use tracing paper to play with bubble plan ideas. Tracing paper is available at art supply stores.

Make sure to include the other members of your household in this important planning step. They'll be enthusiastic about the work if you've included everyone in the planning process.

Sketch the landscape features you're considering on a photocopy or tracing paper copy of your site map. Feel free to experiment; it costs nothing to dream.

You can test different bubble plans in your yard by outlining features with stakes and string. You can use cardboard cutouts to represent stepping-stones and walkways.

Creating a Landscape Design

Once your bubble plan experiments have yielded a plan you like, it's time to turn it into a formal landscape design. The landscape design will serve as a road map for your future landscape. It's particularly helpful if you have a big landscape renovation planned that will take several seasons to complete.

The landcape design can be a chance to have some artistic fun. You can illustrate your design in color, if you want. You may have a few false starts, so it will help to have several copies of your final site map when you begin.

The key to a professional-looking design is to use smooth flowing lines rather than straight lines and sharp angles. Aim for a feeling of continuous flow through the different areas of your landscape. In the final design, the boundaries of the spaces should resemble the rounded flowing lines of your bubble plan.

On a fresh copy of your site map, outline the hardscape features, including patio or deck surfaces, fences, walls, hedges, garden areas, and pathways.

Add symbols and textures for any remaining elements, then use colored pencils to finish the design.

Creating Working Drawings

The final step of this planning process is the starting point for the actual projects you'll find on the pages of this book. Working drawings are individual plans for specific projects within your overall landscape. If you happen to be working from a pre-existing plan, such as a deck or gazebo blueprint, you may not need to make your own drawings. If you're designing your own project, though, making working drawings is what will let you estimate materials and organize your steps.

Working plans serve the same function for landscape construction as blueprints do for builders creating a house. The working plan is a bare-bones version of a plan drawing that includes only the measurements and specifications needed to actually create the project.

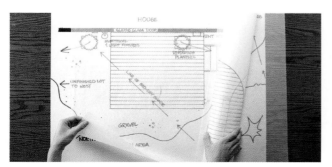

On an enlargment of your landscape design, or using tracing paper, make a more detailed overhead view of the specific project, showing structural measurements.

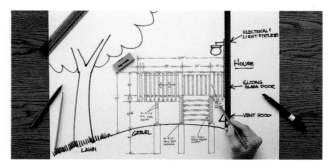

Create detailed plan and elevation drawings for your project. List all dimensions on the drawing, and indicate size, type, and quantities of lumber and hardware needed.

Green Landscapes ▸

As any backyard gardener knows, getting things to grow involves a great deal of trial and error . . . and also time, money, patience, and even wonder: How can it be that your next-door neighbor has more perfect tomatoes than she knows what to do with when all you can produce is a handful of mealy specimens each year? It could be her soil or her technique, but most likely the difference is that her backyard's microclimate is a better environment for growing tomatoes.

In the bigger picture, this imbalance occurs not just across the globe but also from county to county. Yet, you can visit any garden center in, say, Colorado, and find a huge selection of plants that evolved not on the Western plains but in coastal climates or even the dampest regions of Scotland. These plants may survive in the dry Colorado air with enormous amounts of irrigation and probably lots of chemicals, but it begs the question: Why fight nature?

Choosing plants that are well-adapted to the local climate (and your yard's microclimate) is the first step in creating a green landscape, both literally and figuratively. In many regions, this also means limiting the amount of conventional grass because of its insatiable thirst for water. The next step is to look for ways to use water more efficiently and for collecting free water when Mother Nature provides it (good luck to those of you in Colorado and the Southwest).

When it comes to the manmade elements of the landscape, the basic precepts of green building apply: Choose renewable, recyclable, and healthful materials such as recycled-plastic decking and locally produced mulch. Also consider permeable paving in place of concrete and asphalt to keep storm runoff in the ground instead of loading up the sewer system with water and all the yard and driveway chemicals it brings with it. In this illustration you'll find some of the features you'll find in a well-planned, low-maintenance landscape.

A green yard tends to look very natural and very at-home in its surroundings. It should be populated with native plants that don't require heroic efforts to thrive and it should require little or no watering or chemical fertilization. Ideally, a green yard also has a positive impact on your home and property by providing valuable shade or preventing soil erosion.

ELEMENTS OF A GREEN YARD

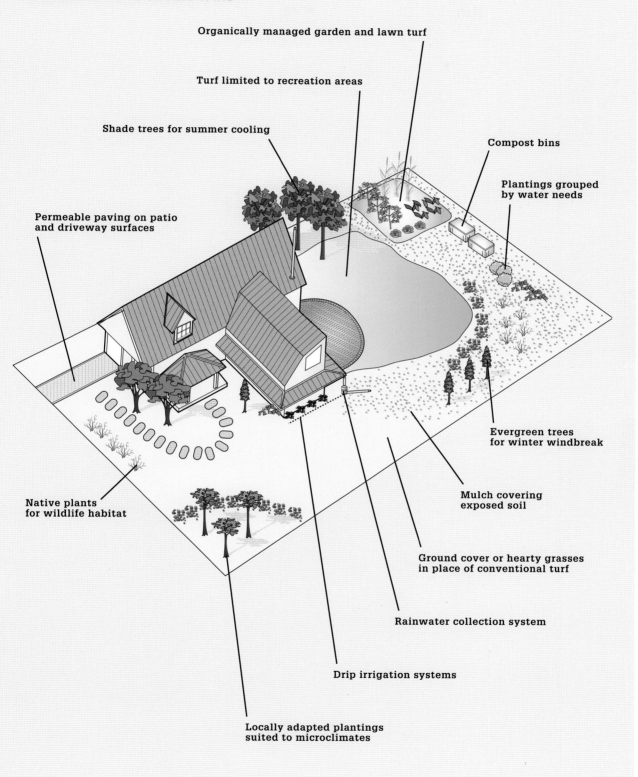

Organically managed garden and lawn turf

Turf limited to recreation areas

Shade trees for summer cooling

Compost bins

Plantings grouped by water needs

Permeable paving on patio and driveway surfaces

Native plants for wildlife habitat

Evergreen trees for winter windbreak

Mulch covering exposed soil

Ground cover or hearty grasses in place of conventional turf

Rainwater collection system

Drip irrigation systems

Locally adapted plantings suited to microclimates

Landscaping with Earth

These projects are the foundation of your landscape design, and that includes changing the shape of your terrain, clearing areas, planting large specimens, and creating dramatic beds. All of these projects involve digging and somehow altering the physical form of your landscape, whether by creating a dry bed of natural stone such as an Arroyo, or by building raised garden beds so you can plant a bountiful herb garden. The work you complete in these projects will change your yard's structure and feel by improving drainage, preventing wind damage, adding privacy with trees, and installing mechanicals like lighting.

In this chapter:

- Gallery
- Grading Your Yard
- Lawn Renovation
- Clearing Brush
- Creating a Windbreak
- Building Raised Beds
- Arroyo
- Swales
- Landscape Bed & Patio Edging
- Low-voltage Landscape Lighting

Gallery

Rolling land has charm and character that can be enhanced by the addition of well-sited fences, walls and structures. If your property is flatter than you'd like, you may be able to create berms and terraces with earth, but take care that you don't cause any drainage problems in the process.

A few prominent rocks placed in a lush planting bed add contrasting textures and, depending on the type, size and accessibility, can even provide a perch from which the plant life can be observed and enjoyed.

Retaining wall blocks can be used to create flat terraces in hilly lawns, making them more usable. They can also make a flat yard look more interesting when they're used to create planting beds that are well integrated into the landscape. Used with some restraint, ornamental yard accessories heighten visual interest and make your yard unique. Some, such as this birdbath and birdfeeder, have a purpose that goes beyond simply being decorative.

Add a hardscaping element to create a buffer between two parts of the yard that have little in common visually. The loose-laid flagstone pathway seen here softens the overall look of the yard by tying the perennial bed to the lawn and planting area.

Create an inviting, usable yard area by clearing brush and leveling the ground in and around a pre-existing landscape feature, such as this stand of maples.

Repeating shapes in your garden is a fun way to draw your guests into the surroundings, as this birds-eye view reveals.

Planting shorter plants in the front of a planting bed and increasing height as you move away is a common landscaping technique. You may find, however, that reversing the two can have a surprising effect that you find pleasing.

Some creative work with your pruning shears can have entertaining results in your landscape. Tall arborvitae, boxwood hedgerows and ornamental shrubs co-exist nicely in this well-tended yard.

Loose gravel pathways look very natural in any landscape, plus they have the added benefit of helping to channel and control water runoff. Here, gravel and river rock are layered into a drainage swale to make the area walkable without negatively affecting its drainage role.

Grading Your Yard

The indicators that your property may need some re-grading work can be subtle, but because the effects are usually troublesome it pays to examine your yard carefully and correct any problems you discover. You may not realize the reason that you have difficulty growing grass and plants is because an "off" grade ushers water into low-lying areas of your property, causing boggy zones that drown plant life. And a poor grade is often the culprit behind a perpetually wet basement. When land slopes toward the foundation of a home, water run-off follows this path to the base of the house. You can solve these issues by grading your yard correctly, which means achieving a gradual slope away from the house of about ¾ inch per horizontal foot.

Generally, a landscape contractor manages the initial grading of a yard, but you can do the work yourself to save money. The job is time-consuming and a bit labor-intensive, but it isn't especially complicated. In most cases, you'll start with a four-inch to six-inch layer of topsoil to spread over the yard so you can fill in sunken areas and smooth out gradual slopes. Your goal is to establish a grade that controls runoff by sloping gently away from the house.

Tools & Materials ▸

Line level	Tape
Grading rake	Hand tamp
Stakes	Topsoil
Shovels	Wheelbarrow
String	

A skid loader or a comparable compact earthmoving vehicle is essential for large re-grading projects. Generally, homeowners are well advised to hire professional landscapers for groundwork that requires more than a shovel and a garden rake to accomplish.

Leveling a Yard ▸

If you want a perfectly flat surface for playing sports or to create a play surface for children, outline the perimeter of this area with evenly placed stakes. Extend a string fitted with a line level between a pair of stakes and adjust the string until it's level. At 2-ft. intervals, measure down from the marked areas of the string to the ground. Add and remove topsoil as necessary, distributing it with a garden rake until the surface under the string is level. Repeat the process until the area is level.

How to Measure and Establish a Grade

Drive a stake into the soil at the base of the foundation and another at least 8 ft. out into the yard along a straight line from the first stake. Attach a string fitted with a line level to the stakes and level it. Measure and flag the string with tape at 1-ft. intervals. Measure down from the string at the tape flags, recording your measurements to use as guidelines for adding or removing soil to create a correct grade.

Working away from the base of the house, add soil to low areas until they reach the desired height. Using a garden rake, evenly distribute the soil over a small area. Measure down from the 1-ft. markings as you work to make sure that you are creating a ¾" per 1 ft. pitch. Add and remove soil as needed until soil is evenly sloped, then move on to the next area and repeat the process.

Use a hand tamp to lightly compact the soil. Don't overtamp the soil or it could become too dense to grow a healthy lawn or plants.

After all the soil is tamped, use a grading rake to remove any rocks or clumps. Starting at the foundation, pull the rake in a straight line down the slope. Dispose of any rocks or construction debris. Repeat the process, working on one section at a time until the entire area around the house is graded.

Lawn Renovation

If your lawn is a teenager—say 15 years old, or so—it might be time to give the yard a fresh start by renovating it. Over time, thatch buildup can choke out healthy grass and promote weeds and disease. Thatch is a layer of partially decomposed grass stems, roots, and rhizomes at the soil surface. An indication of too much thatch is a spongy, soft lawn that doesn't take well to watering and fertilizers.

Other symptoms of a lawn that needs renovation include dead spots or areas of sparse growth, which can be due to infertile soil, drought, insect damage, poor mowing practices, disease, soil compaction, or too much shade. Generally speaking, if 20 to 40 percent of your lawn is dead or dying, you can remedy the problem through lawn renovation. If more than 40 percent of your lawn is in dire condition, you will need to reseed or re-sod your lawn.

Thatch hides below the grass surface, so you may need to cut out a 6"-deep wedge so you can measure the level of thatch. If you can see that the thatch is deeper than ½", then you've got some lawn renovation to do.

First, Diagnose the Problem

Before you begin the lawn renovation process, determine why your lawn is failing. Once you identify the cause, you can take corrective action during the renovation process and start fresh with proper cultural practices such as mowing, fertilizing, and watering as soon as the process is complete. Careful observation and taking soil samples for analysis can shed light on what's ailing your lawn.

Some of the diagnostic questions you'll need to ask are: How thick is the thatch (see photo above)? How much of your lawn is overtaken with weeds? What weather conditions (heat, drought, excessive moisture) might have contributed to the lawn's condition? The fix might be as simple as trimming back a tree canopy that's preventing a patch of your lawn from receiving adequate sunlight. Usually, the problem stems from a variety of issues: thatch and an insect problem, plus a dry summer—you get the idea.

A soil test is the best way to get to the root of a lawn problem. By collecting soil samples and testing the soil pH level, which is its acidity and alkalinity, you'll have the information you need to feed the soil nutrients to help repair the lawn.

Testing Your Soil ▸

You'll have greater success growing healthy plants and groundcover if you test your soil and amend it based on the test results. You can purchase soil test kits at garden stores, or you can send a sample to a university extension for testing. Collect small soil samples from several different spots in your yard. Mix these samples together, then send a portion of it to the lab. Most labs provide a testing kit with a calibrated vial to contain the blended soil sample. Soil reports vary quite a bit in their thoroughness, but a typical report from an agriculture extension will note soil texture, pH level, and levels of essential nutrients, including nitrogen, potassium, and phosphorous. The report also will suggest fertilizer types and spread rates.

How to Collect Soil Samples

Collect small soil samples from several spots in your yard, and from multiple depths. You can use a shovel, trowel, or even a spoon to collect the samples. Or, you can purchase a soil probe that will give you neat samples with minimal disturbance to the surrounding turf.

Mix the soil samples together in a small, clean plastic bucket. Blend the samples thoroughly. You may get a sample bag from a laboratory for this purpose. Prepare the sample by loading the specified amount of soil into the vial or bag provided with your kit.

Complete the lab order form, indicating which plants you intend to grow. A basic test will provide your soil pH level and other information you need to determine whether your soil needs amendments.

Option: Use an instant-read tester to find and monitor the pH level in your soil.

Prepare the Site

Before you rent a power aerator or vigorously rake thatch from your lawn, prepare the site by removing weeds and replenishing soil moisture (if dry). You'll have a tough time aerating or dethatching. Depending on the type and number of weeds, you can physically remove them or you can use a selective or nonselective herbicide to wipe out the unwanteds. For instance, if weeds are primarily broad-leaved, you can use a broad leaf herbicide on the entire lawn. (Then, wait two to four weeks before overseeding.) If crabgrass or patches of weeds are a problem, consider treating the spots with a nonselective herbicide that will kill all of the growth in that area. Be careful to protect the surrounding, healthy lawn. As its name indicates, nonselective herbicides don't discriminate when they kill off growth. Always follow label instructions and wear proper safety gear, including eye and hand protection.

The best time of year to renovate your lawn is in the fall. But in many regions, this is also the time when lawns are most parched after a hot, dry summer. Replenishing moisture is an important step prior to dethatching, aerating, and overseeding a lawn. If the ground is too dry, the job will be more physically demanding as you try to loosen hard ground, and less effective because seed will not establish in a dusty soil profile. Soil should be moist to a depth of six inches before you begin working it, which could take days to achieve. Don't rush this process.

Establish a Healthy Lawn

Removing thatch doesn't have to be a back-breaking chore if you use power equipment such as a vertical mower (also called a verticutter) or an aerator. These two machines operate quite differently, but they can both accomplish the goal of loosening thatch from soil and creating more breathing room for healthy turf to receive water and sunlight so it will thrive. A vertical mower works by pushing tines into the soil surface to a depth of ⅛ to ½ inch. These tines pull up thatch in clumps, which then can be raked away. An aerator removes soil plugs, leaving cores of soil on the lawn that can be left to dry and break down back into the soil. If you choose to aerate a lawn with heavy thatch, go over the lawn three to five times and allow soil plugs to dry (or remove them) before overseeding.

You may decide to hire a professional to verticut or aerate your lawn. This equipment is also available for rent, so if you partner up with a neighbor, you can split the cost and share the aerator or verticutter for a day. You'll save time and your back by preparing the lawn by machine. Dethatching by hand is best for small areas.

Seasonal maintenance is an important ingredient to a healthy yard. Leaf collection in the fall and a gentle raking in the spring (after grass plants have reestablished) will allow air to feed the plants.

Lawn Renovation Tips

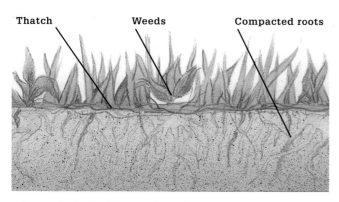

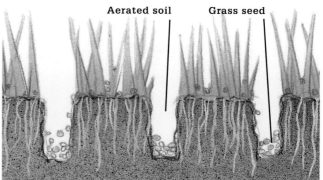

A lawn choked with weeds and excess thatch (left) will be more prone to bare spots and brown patches. Weed abatement, thatch removal, aeration, and reseeding create the proper conditions for healthy lawn growth (right).

Repairing Bare Spots ▸

If your lawn is plagued with dying areas, you'll need to determine the cause and take preventive measures to keep the grass from dying again. Once the problem is solved, sprinkle grass seed over the bare area, lightly rake it into the soil, and gently tamp the soil down. Keep the area moist for at least two weeks while the seed germinates. Use the following guidelines to resolve common problems:

CAUSE	SOLUTION
Dog damage	Immediately water areas where the dog urinates.
Compacted soil	Aerate the area, or till in an amendment, such as compost or peat moss.
Chemical burn	Remove several inches of topsoil from the bare area.
Disease	Consult your local extension service for diagnosis and treatment.
Foot traffic	Install a path or stepping stones to accommodate traffic.
Insects	Consult your local extension service for recommendations.

Reading Grass Seed Container Labels ▸

The type of grass you select will play a large part in the success of your lawn. But it can be difficult to tell exactly what you're buying. Whether it's a prepackaged blend or seed sold by the pound in bulk, there will always be a label that tells you exactly what type of seeds are included in that blend.

PURE SEED	VARIETY	GERMINATION
42%	Colonel Kentucky Bluegrass	88%
33%	Fine Perennial Ryegrass	78%
21%	Red Tall Fescue	80%
0.4%	Inert Matter	
1.2%	Crop	
2.4%	Weed	

Pure Seed: the percentage of seeds for each variety that are capable of growing.
Germination: the portion of the pure seed that will germinate within a reasonable amount of time.
Inert Matter: materials present in the blend, such as broken seeds, hulls, and chaff, that aren't capable of growing.
Crop: the percentage of agricultural grain and undesirable grass seed contained in the blend.
Weed: the portion of weed seeds present in the blend.

How to Renovate a Lawn

Spot-treat weeds by applying selective herbicides using a pressure sprayer. Use a broadleaf herbicide to treat weeds such as dandelion and clover. Choose a nonselective herbicide for crabgrass and quackgrass. Be careful to protect healthy turf.

Remove thatch with a vertical mower. Set tines to rake ⅛" to ½" below the surface of the soil. Push the mower in straight passes. Then make a second pass over the entire lawn working in a perpendicular direction to the first passes. Cover the area in a grid pattern. Rake up and discard removed thatch.

Use an aerator to alleviate soil compaction and improve drainage by removing small cores of soil from the lawn. Run the machine across your lawn using the grid pattern described in step 2. Allow soil cores to dry partially, then rake them up. (Some can be left to decompose completely.) Follow by using a vertical mower or leaf rake to scratch and loosen the surface.

Use a broadcast spreader with a fertilizer blend (refer to soil report for appropriate NPK ratio). Calibrate the spreader according to instructions on the fertilizer package. Distribute the fertilizer evenly across the lawn. Fertilizer may need to be watered in before seeding. Follow by filling spreader with seed and distributing evenly.

How to Repair Lawn Damage

Moisten the damaged area, and use a garden fork to break up the soil. Rake out dead grass or other debris.

Spread grass seed over the repair area. Select seed that matches the grass type in your lawn—this often is a blend of several different types. Broadcast the seed at the coverage rate recommended on the package.

Fertilize the new grass plants with a grass seed starter formulation. Again, use the coverage rate specified on the package.

Water the repair area thoroughly, but not so much that you cause fertilizer granules or seeds to wash away. Install stakes and strings around the repair area to discourage foot traffic. Water the area daily until the new grass has established.

Clearing Brush

Nuisance trees, invasive plants, and thorny groundcovers latch on to your land and form a vegetative barrier, greatly limiting the usefulness of a space. Before you can even think of the patio plan or garden plot you wish to place in that space, you'll need to clear the way. If the area is a sea of thorny brush or entirely wooded, you'll probably want to hire an excavator, logger, or someone with heavy-duty bulldozing equipment to manage the job. But on suburban plots, brush can usually be cleared without the need for major machinery.

Dress for protection when taking on a brush-clearing job. You never know what mysteries and challenges reside on your property behind the masses of branches and bramble. Wear boots, long pants, gloves, long sleeves, and eye protection. Follow a logical workflow when clearing brush—generally, clean out the tripping hazards first so you can access the bigger targets more safely.

Tools & Materials ▸

Pruners	Landscape fabric
Loppers	(optional)
Bow saw	Safety glasses
Weed cutter	Gloves
Nonselective	Long sleeves
herbicide (optional)	and pants

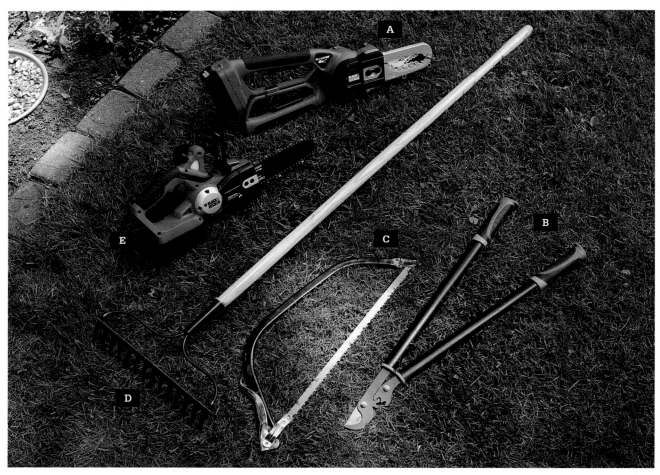

Cutting and removal tools used for brush clearing should be scaled for the job you're asking them to do. Simple hand tools can handle much of the work, but for bigger jobs having the right power tools is a tremendous worksaver. Tools shown here include: electric lopper (cordless) (A); loppers (B); bow saw (C); garden (bow) rake (D); chainsaw (cordless) (E).

How to Clear Brush

Begin by using a tree pruner to cut woody brush that has a diameter of less than 1½". Cut the brush and/or small trees as close to the ground as possible, dragging brush out of the way and into a pile as you clear.

Next, clear out larger plants—brush and trees with a diameter of about 1½" to 3½". Use a bow saw or chain saw to cut through the growth, and place the debris in a pile. Trees larger than 4" diameter should be left to grow, or removed under the supervision of a professional.

Use a heavy-duty string trimmer or a swing-blade style weed cutter to cut tangled shoots, weeds, and remaining underbrush from the area.

Clear the cut debris and dispose of it immediately. Curbside pickup of yardwaste usually requires that sticks or branches be tied up into bundles no more than 3 ft. long. If you plan to install a hardscape surface, make sure the brush does not grow back by using a nonselective herbicide to kill off remaining shoots or laying landscape fabric.

Creating a Windbreak

Wind saps heat from homes, forces snow into burdensome drifts, and can damage more tender plants in a landscape. To protect your outdoor living space, build an aesthetically pleasing wall—a "green" wall of tress and shrubs—that will cut the wind and keep those energy bills down. Windbreaks are commonly used in rural areas where sweeping acres of land are a runway for wind gusts. But even those on small, suburban lots will benefit from strategically placing plants to block the wind.

Essentially, windbreaks are plantings or screens that slow, direct, and block wind from protected areas. Natural windbreaks are comprised of shrubs, conifers, and deciduous trees. The keys to a successful windbreak are: height, width, density, and orientation. Height and width come with age. Density depends on the number of rows, type of foliage, and gaps. Ideally, a windbreak should be 60 to 80 percent dense. (No windbreak is 100 percent dense.) Orientation involves placing rows of plants at right angles to the wind. A rule of thumb is to plant a windbreak that is ten times longer than its greatest height. And keep in mind that wind changes direction, so you may need a multiple-leg windbreak.

Tools & Materials ▶

Shovel
Garden hose
Utility knife

Trees
Soil amendments
(as needed)

A stand of fast-growing trees, like these aspens, will create an effective windbreak for your property just a few years after saplings are planted.

Windbreak Benefits ▶

Windbreaks deliver multiple benefits to your property.
Energy conservation: reduce energy costs from 20 to 40 percent.
Snow control: single rows of shrubs function as snow fences.
Privacy: block a roadside view and protect animals from exposure to passers-by.
Noise control: muffle the sound of traffic if your pasture or home is near a road.
Aesthetic appeal: improve your landscape and increase the value of your property.
Erosion control: prevent dust from blowing; roots work against erosion.

How to Plant a Windbreak

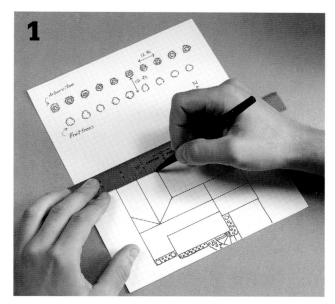

Before you pick up a shovel, draw a plan of your windbreak, taking into consideration the direction of the wind and location of nearby structures. Windbreaks can be straight lines of trees or curved formations. They may be several rows thick, or just a single row. If you only have room for one row, choose lush evergreens for the best density. Make a plan.

Once you decide on the best alignment of trees and shrubs, stake out reference lines for the rows. For a three-row windbreak, the inside row should be at least 75 ft. from buildings or structures, with the outside row 100 to 150 ft. away. Within this 25 to 75 ft. area, plant rows 16 to 20 ft. apart for shrubs and conifers and no closer than 14 ft. for deciduous trees. Within rows, space trees so their foliage can mature and eventually improve the density.

Dig holes for tree root balls to the recommended depth (see pages 86 to 87). Your plan should arrange short trees or shrubs upwind and taller trees downwind. If your windbreak borders your home, choose attractive plants for the inside row and buffer them with evergreens or dense shrubs in the second row. If you only have room for two rows of plants, be sure to stagger the specimens so there are no gaps.

Plant the trees in the formation created in your plan. Follow the tree and shrub planting techniques on pages 86 to 87. Here, a row of dwarf fruit trees is being planted in front of a row of denser, taller evergreens (Techny Arborvitae).

Building Raised Beds

Raised beds are convenient homes for vegetables, herbs, and flowers. You can establish the perfect growing environment and maintain healthy soil easily in a raised bed. Home gardeners everywhere are raising up their beds because this method of planting is versatile, productive, and convenient. Even better news: these structures are not too difficult to build.

In raised beds, soil does not suffer compaction from foot traffic. Also, you can better control soil pH, which explains why gardeners report higher production yields in raised beds: about 0.6 pounds of vegetables per square foot, or more. Another bonus: You can easily water plants in raised beds with soaker hoses, which deliver water to soil and roots rather than spraying leaves and inviting disease.

Generally, raised beds are no wider than four feet, which allows you to easily reach from one side to the middle without climbing in to care for plants. You can extend raised beds for as long as you please. Position beds at north-south orientation for low-growing crops so both sides of the bed gain exposure to direct sunlight. Taller crops thrive when positioned east-west. A system of beds can face different directions, depending on what you plant in them. Frames or borders are optional, but make for a nice, neat bed that contains soil and helps keep critters out.

Tools & Materials ▸

Spade	Roofing nails
Reciprocating saw or power miter saw	Landscape fabric or EPDM roofing membrane
Drill and drill-driver	
Painting equipment	Topsoil
Stakes and string	Plantings
4 × 4 landscape timbers	Exterior paint or wood-sealer protectant
6" galvanized nails	
10" timber screws	

Raised planting beds are easy to make from landscape lumber. In addition to elevating the plants so they're easier to reach, raised beds keep plants and leaves from spreading, limit diseases, and allow you to more easily customize your soil amendments. A colorful raised bed also provides yard decoration in nongrowing seasons.

How to Build a Raised Planting Bed

Dig with a shovel to remove grass inside a rectangle that was measured and outlined with stakes and string. Then, dig a trench for the first row of timbers.

Lay and level the first layer of timbers in the trench. Once level, set down the second, staggering the joints. Drill holes at each corner and drive nails through the holes. Or, drive long timber screws to draw the joints together.

Place and secure the third layer of landscape timbers over the second, staggering the joints. Drill ½" drainage holes through the bottom row of the timbers. Line the walls and bottom of the raised bed with landscape fabric. *Option: Add a cap of 2 × 6 or 2 × 8 treated lumber for visual appeal and to create a more comfortable working surface. Fill the bed with topsoil, peat and compost, then plant your garden.*

Cross-section of a Raised Bed ▸

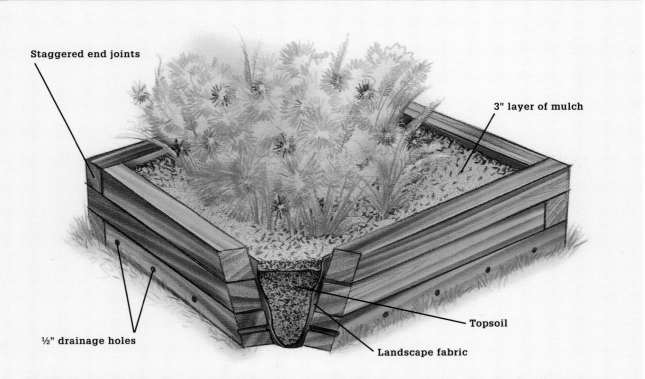

Staggered end joints

3" layer of mulch

½" drainage holes

Landscape fabric

Topsoil

Raised beds do not need to be contained within frames or borders, but for smaller beds within a defined landscape, some kind of border improves the appearance and keeps the garden from migrating into the surrounding lawn.

Choosing a Raised Garden Theme

Raised beds offer an opportunity to create specific garden panting themes. If you envision bouquets of fresh flowers from spring through fall, a cutting garden with a variety of annuals and perennials will provide the bounty required to fill your home with fresh flowers. If you wish to attract beautiful butterflies to watch, plant a selection of nectar-producing plants with overlapping blooming periods. Kitchen-gardeners will want to pick fresh herbs for cooking—a farm-to-table movement right in your backyard. Take edibles to a higher level and dedicate a raised bed for vegetables. You'll find it is easier to put a raised bed "to bed" at the end of the season. All you need is some basic tools to trowel up spent plants, and a cover, such as a tarp, to protect the soil during the winter.

A square raised garden includes a collection of common herbs. Even in a raised bed, ornaments like this ceramic birdbath add character and boost the entertainment factor for bird watchers.

Herb Garden

Some herbs are annuals and require planting each year. Others are biennials that live two seasons and bloom the second season. Perennials bloom each season. Start out with a bed of healthy soil by tilling and adding soil amendments such as compost or peat moss if necessary. Herbs thrive in raised beds, so you'll have plenty of fragrant bounty to preserve for winter or give to neighbors and friends.

Keep in mind when choosing herbs, plants are classified as annuals and perennials depending on their zones. A plant rated as "Perennial in Zone 10," won't tolerate temperatures colder than 30 to 40 degrees Fahrenheit. If you live in a cold climate, this plant functionally becomes an annual because it will die in winter.

Planting an Herb Garden ▶

1. Basil, Ocimum basilicum
2. Broadleaf English thyme, Thymus vulgaris
3. Narrow-leaf French thyme, Thymus vulagaris 'Narrow Leaf French'
4. Garden sage, Salvia
5. Chives, Allium schoenoprasum
6. Silver-edge thyme, Thymus argentia
7. Golden lemon thyme, Thymus citriodorus
8. Greek oregano, Origanum heracleoticum
9. Sweet marjoram, Majorana hortensis
10. Rosemary (potted), Rosmarinus officinalis
11. German chamomile, Matricaria recutita
12. Parsley, Petroselinum crispum
13. Bee balm, Monarda didyma
14. Lemon verbena, Aloysia triphylla
15. Pineapple sage, Salvia elegans
16. Mexican marigold mint, Tagetes lucida
17. French tarragon, Artemisia dracunculus
18. Slate stepping stones
19. Bird bath

Butterfly Garden

Butterflies are nature's ballet company. The delicate creatures flutter about, dance in sunlight, which they love, and pose gracefully on petal tips, sipping sweet drinks of their favorite elixir: nectar. You can encourage butterflies to visit your garden by planting flowers rich in this substance. We'll show you how to create a habitat so you can lure in butterflies and persuade them to stay in your yard so you can enjoy the show.

Attract Butterflies ▸

The perfect environment to attract butterflies includes these factors: a variety of annuals and perennials, sun spots, shade areas, puddles, and a feeder. Common plants that butterflies like include:

Aster, Astrum
Black-eyed Susan, Thunbergia alata
Butterfly weed, Asclepias tuberose
Coreopsis, Coreopsis tinctoria
Black Dalea, Dalea frutescens
Daylilies, Hemerocallis
Goldenrod, Solidago odora
Hibiscus, Hibiscus moscheutos
Lavender, Lavandula
Lilac, Syringa vulgaris
Marigold, Calendula officinalis
Nasturtium, Tropaeolum majus
Peony, Paeonia
Petunia, Petunia x hybrida
Redbud, Cercis occidentalis
Rosemary, Rosmarinus
Verbena, Verbena

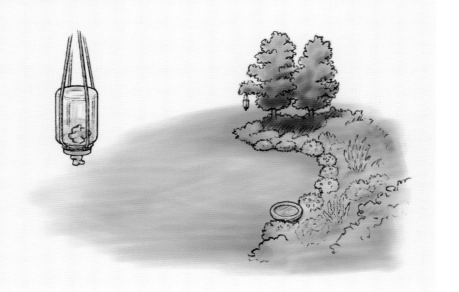

How to Plant a Butterfly Garden

Provide plants butterflies are attracted to (see list above). Plant different sizes and flowers with various blooms in an area with some trees or shrubs to provide cover (shade areas), and some open spaces that allow light exposure (sun spots).

Provide a water source for butterflies. Make puddles by burying a planter saucer into the plant bed, covering the brim. Fill the saucer with gravel or sand before filling with water, a sweet drink, or stale beer. Supplement the puddle with a feeder.

Arroyo

An arroyo is a dry streambed or watercourse in an arid climate that directs water runoff on the rare occasions when there is a downfall. In a home landscape an arroyo may be used for purely decorative purposes, with the placement of stones evoking water where the real thing is scarce. Or it may serve a vital water-management function, directing storm runoff away from building foundations to areas where it may percolate into the ground and irrigate plants, creating a great spot for a rain garden. This water management function is becoming more important as municipalities struggle with an overload of storm sewer water, which can degrade water quality in rivers and lakes. Some communities now offer tax incentives to homeowners who keep water out of the street.

When designing your dry streambed, keep it natural and practical. Use local stone that's arranged as it would be found in a natural stream. Take a field trip to an area containing natural streams and make some observations. Note how quickly the water depth drops at the outside of bends where only larger stones can withstand the current. By the same token, note how gradually the water level drops at the inside of broad bends where water movement is slow. Place smaller river-rock gravel here, as it would accumulate in a natural stream.

Large heavy stones with flat tops may serve as step stones, allowing paths to cross or even follow dry stream beds.

The most important design standard with dry streambeds is to avoid regularity. Stones are never spaced evenly in nature and nor should they be in your arroyo. If you dig a bed with consistent width, it will look like a canal or a drainage ditch, not a stream. And consider other yard elements and furnishings. For example, an arroyo presents a nice opportunity to add a landscape bridge or two to your yard.

An arroyo is a drainage swale lined with rocks that directs runoff water from a point of origin, such as a gutter downspout, to a destination, such as a sewer drain or a rain garden.

Important: Contact your local waste management bureau before routing water toward a storm sewer; this may be illegal.

Tools & Materials ▸

Landscape paint	Wheelbarrow	8"-thick steppers	Native grasses or other
Carpenter's level	Landscape fabric	6 to 18" dia.	perennials for banks
Spades	6-mil black plastic	river-rock boulders	Eye protection
Garden rake	Mulch	¾ to 2" river rock	Work gloves

How to Build an Arroyo

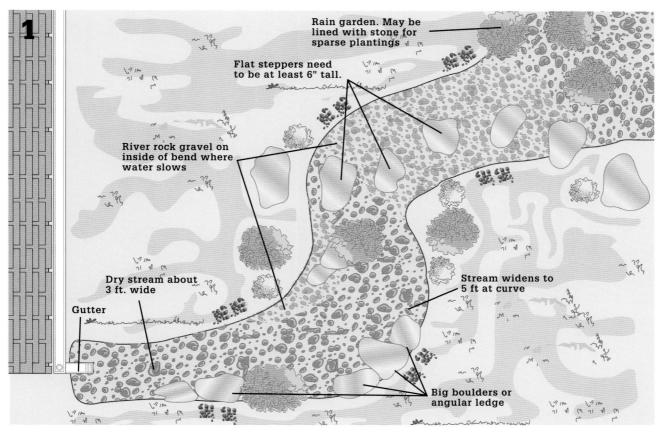

1

Rain garden. May be lined with stone for sparse plantings

Flat steppers need to be at least 6" tall.

River rock gravel on inside of bend where water slows

Dry stream about 3 ft. wide

Gutter

Stream widens to 5 ft at curve

Big boulders or angular ledge

Create a plan for the arroyo. The best designs have a very natural shape and a rock distribution strategy that mimics the look of a stream. Arrange a series of flat steppers at some point to create a bridge.

Lay out the dry stream bed, following the native topography of your yard as much as possible. Mark the borders and then step back and review it from several perspectives.

Excavate the soil to a depth of at least 12" (30 cm) in the arroyo area. Use the soil you dig up to embellish or repair your yard.

(continued)

Widen the arroyo in selected areas to add interest. Rake and smooth out the soil in the project area.

Install an underlayment of landscape fabric over the entire dry streambed. Keep the fabric loose so you have room to manipulate it later if the need arises.

Set larger boulders at outside bends in the arroyo. Imagine that there is a current to help you visualize where the individual stones could naturally end up.

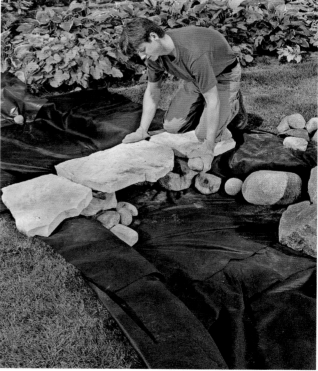

Place flagstone steppers or boulders with relatively flat surfaces in a stepping-stone pattern to make a pathway across the arroyo (left photo). Alternately, create a "bridge" in an area where you're likely to be walking (right photo).

8

Add more stones, including steppers and medium-size landscape boulders. Use smaller aggregate to create the stream bed, filling in and around, but not covering, the larger rocks.

9

Dress up your new arroyo by planting native grasses and perennials around its banks.

What is a Rain Garden? ▸

A rain garden is simply a shallow, wide depression at least ten feet away from a basement foundation that collects storm water runoff. Rain gardens are planted with native flood-tolerant plants and typically hold water for only hours after rainfall. Check your local garden center or Extension Service to find details about creating rain gardens in your area.

Swales

If your yard is beginning to look like a boggy mess because of low-lying areas that collect water run-off, a drainage swale is just the solution to control wet zones. Swales work much like rain gardens: Both are designed to direct water run-off to an area of capture so water can slowly drain back into the soil or be redirected to an appropriate outlet, such as a storm water sewer. The difference is, a swale is basically a shallow, vegetated collection trench and a rain garden requires establishing an entire drainage environment. Depending on the run-off severity, a simple swale might be all you'll need to keep your lawn from turning into swampland.

Just because a swale is a practical ditch doesn't mean it can't enhance the landscape's overall look. Resist the urge to dig a trench, fill with sod, and leave it at that. Think of your swale as a creek environment without the rushing water. What type of surroundings would you expect along a riverbed? Natural stone gives a swale area a rustic appeal. Plant grasses over the swale trench and treat the berm as a plant bed for perennials or native grasses. These finishing touches will ensure the swale is a beauty mark on your landscape and not an eyesore.

As you plan the swale, also keep in mind that the swale should be positioned slightly uphill from your drainage zone. A swale cannot usually run in an unbroken line because it must be dug on contour and have a level bottom so water will pool evenly and seep deep into the bed. You may need to build a system of swales—two or three that run a horizontal line but are placed at slightly different positions on the slope. The swale we'll build in this project is a single trench that's six inches deep. A swale should be half as deep as it is wide, so this swale will be one foot wide.

If you are building a swale between your house and the property next door, talk to your neighbor about the project beforehand. If drainage is a problem for them as well, they might be willing to split the cost or team up to build the swale. If the thought of labor-intensive digging will send you to the phone book to call a professional—go ahead. Or, simply rent a trencher or backhoe for the day to get the job done faster. You'll still need a shovel for leveling and finishing the trench.

Note: Before beginning, have your public utility flag any electrical, gas or plumbing lines in or near the project area.

Tools & Materials ▸

Hammer or maul   Shovel
Wheelbarrow   Work gloves
Spade   Stakes
Spading fork   Landscape fabric
Sod cutter (optional)   Coarse gravel

EcoTip ▸

A swale can double as a water filter if you install plants with well-established root systems along the entrance area to "clean" water as it runs off into the trench. Grasses planted in the swale dip will clean run-off water (so long as you avoid using chemical lawn care products on this land) before it reaches storm sewers.

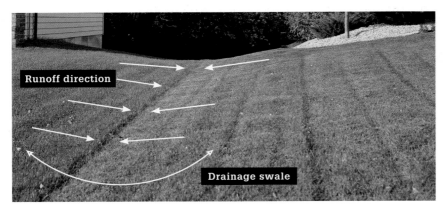

Runoff direction

Drainage swale

Improve drainage in a large low-lying area by creating a shallow ditch, called a drainage swale, to carry runoff water away. If your region receives frequent heavy rainfalls or if you have dense soil that drains poorly, you may need to lay a perforated drainpipe and a bed of gravel under the swale to make it more effective (see next page).

Swale Options

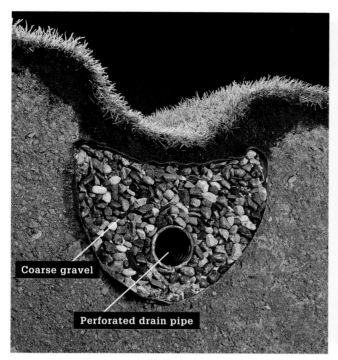

Coarse gravel

Perforated drain pipe

Splash block

For severe drainage problems, dig a 1-ft. deep swale angled slightly downward to the outlet point. Line the swale with landscape fabric. Spread a 2"-layer of coarse gravel in the bottom of the swale. Then lay perforated drainpipe over the gravel. Cover the pipe with a 5"-layer of gravel and wrap the landscape fabric over the top of it. Cover the swale with soil and fresh sod. Set a splash block at the outlet to distribute the runoff and prevent erosion.

Coarse

Smooth

Gravel comes in two forms: coarse and smooth. When buying gravel for shaping projects, such as drainage swales, select coarse gravel. Coarse gravel clings to the sides of the trench, creating an even drainage layer. Smooth gravel is typically used as a decorative ground cover. When used for shaping projects, it tends to slide toward the middle of the trench.

How to Create a Drainage Swale

Use stakes to mark a swale route that directs water away from the problem area toward a run-off zone. Place stakes slightly uphill from the drainage area.

Remove soil from the marked zone using a shovel. If you must remove grass before digging, consider cutting grass pieces carefully and setting them aside so you can use the turf as sod squares to finish the trench. You can rent or buy a sod cutter to improve your chances of getting reusable cuttings. Otherwise, pile dirt on one side of the trench for a berm.

Shape the trench so it slopes gradually downward toward the outlet, and smooth the sides.

Level the trench by laying a 2 × 4 board with a carpenter's level on the foundation. Distribute soil so the base is level, moving the board to different areas of the trench to check for levelness. Crack the bottom of the swale with a spading fork to aid in percolation (optional).

Lay sod in the trench to complete the swale. Compress the sod and water the area thoroughly to check drainage.

Option: Compact Skidloader

Use the digging attachment on the compact skidloader to move earth. This could mean shearing off the top of a small hill that creates a drainage issue, or excavating to create a natural drainage pattern. Unless you have experience operating utility vehicles, hire a contractor to do this job.

Use a grading attachment on the skidloader to level and move earth. Swales should have very shallow sides and low slopes.

Landscape Bed & Patio Edging

Landscape beds dress up a plain, green yard and provide supple ground for growing perennials, annuals, vegetables, or whatever greenscape you choose to plant. Use your imagination! Beds can be dug to create borders in an outdoor living room, or they may be positioned as "islands" in a sea of green back yard. The shape, size, and location of a landscape bed is really up to you. Then just add edging to add a polished look to any landscape bed, walkway, or patio area. You can trim a bed with brick, natural stone, timber, or even neat-and-clean black plastic edging. Edging serves the practical purpose of containment, keeping surface material in place so it doesn't drift off into the yard. Also, in patio and walkway applications edging can strengthen a curb. Aesthetically speaking, it creates a visual border and provides an opportunity to incorporate hardscape into a landscape design.

Creating Landscape Beds

Planting areas should occupy 40 to 50 percent of your total open yard area, so don't skimp. Think of it this way: More beds means less mowing. Of course, you'll add time to your gardening duties, but if you choose low-maintenance shrubs and perennials that blossom like clockwork each season, the time you spend doting over landscape beds won't steal from other outdoor recreation—like using your outdoor kitchen.

Before you break ground, survey your property and map out where you will place landscape beds. Don't get boxed into linear designs. Experiment with kidney-shaped beds, and beds that seem to flow like a creek with curved edges. Build in border beds that separate outdoor living spaces, such as a patio, from the rest of the yard. Beds also provide privacy when placed along a property line and planted with screening varieties, such as evergreens. (Landscape beds aren't just for flowers, after all.)

Once you decide on bed location and shape, check the soil quality of the area by conducting a soil test. That way you can add the correct soil amendments to be sure you're giving plants the best foundation for growth. Most soil will require amending, and you can do so with organic substances, including: sphagnum peat, wood chips, grass clippings (if you do not use lawn chemicals), straw, or compost. Remember, amendments are mixed into the soil and mulch is placed on the soil, after planting.

In the project shown here, you'll learn how to create a landscape bed with curved edges by using a garden hose to outline the bed shape before you break ground. This bed features plastic edging, which is installed before amending soil. You can choose any number of edging materials (see pages 68 to 73) for this project. As always, before you dig, call your local utilities hotline first.

(see pages 68 to 73)

Tools & Materials ▸

Landscape fabric (optional)	Plants
Soil amendments	Hose
Mulch	Spade
	Shovel

Freeform planting beds within a landscaped yard provide borders, definition, and visual relief.

How to Install a Landscape Bed

Use a garden hose to outline the planned garden bed area. Remove the ground cover inside the area with a spade.

Dig a trench around the perimeter of the bed using a spade. Place plastic lawn edging into the trench and secure it by driving edging stakes into the bottom lip.

Till amendments into the soil with a spade and shovel. Test the design and layout of the plants. Install landscape fabric over the entire area if desired to inhibit weed growth.

Install plant material. Apply a 2" to 3" layer of mulch over the entire surface. Leave 1 to 2" of clearance for tree trunks and woody ornamentals to prevent insects and pests from attacking them.

Rigid Paver Edging

Choose heavy-duty edging that's strong enough to contain your surface materials. If your patio or walkway has curves, buy plenty of notched, or flexible, edging for the curves. Also, buy 12-inch-long galvanized spikes: one for every 12 inches of edging plus extra for curves.

Tools & Materials ▶

Maul
Snips or saw (for
   cutting edging)

Heavy-duty
   plastic edging
12" galvanized spikes

Invisible Edging ▶

Invisible edging is so named for its low-profile edge that stops about halfway up the side edges of pavers. The exposed portion of the edging is easily concealed under soil and sod or groundcover.

Rigid plastic edging installs easily and works well for both curved and straight walkways made from paving stones or brick pavers set in sand.

How to Install Rigid Paver Edging

Set the edging on top of a compacted gravel base covered with landscape fabric. Using your layout strings as guides, secure the edging with spikes driven every 12" (or as recommended by the manufacturer). Along curves, spike the edging at every tab, or as recommended.

Cover the outside of the edging with soil and/or sod after the paving is complete. *Tip: On two or more sides of the patio or path, you can spike the edging minimally, in case you have to make adjustments during the paving. Anchor the edging completely after the paving is done.*

Freeform Paver Edging

Brick edging can be laid in several different configurations (see below): on-end with its edge perpendicular to the paved surface ("soldiers"); on its long edges; or laid flat, either parallel or perpendicular to the paving. For mortared surfaces, brick can also be mortared to the edge of a concrete slab for a decorative finish (see pages 70 to 73 and 160 to 163).

Tools & Materials ▸

Flat shovel
Rubber mallet
2 × 4 (about 12" long)
Bricks
Hand tamper

Garden spade
Work gloves
Gravel
Landscape fabric
Eye protection

Brick Edging Configurations ▸

Brick soldier edging

Brick set on long edges

Brick set on faces, perpendicular or parallel to the patio surface

How to Install Brick Paver Edging

1

Excavate the edge of the patio or walkway site using a flat shovel to create a clean, vertical edge. The edge of the soil (and sod) will support the outsides of the bricks. For edging with bricks set on-end, dig a narrow trench along the perimeter of the site, setting the depth so the tops of the edging bricks will be flush with the paving surface (or just above the surface for loose materials).

2

Set the edging bricks into the trench after installing the gravel subbase and landscape fabric. If applicable, use your layout strings to keep the bricks in line and to check for the proper height. Backfill behind the bricks with soil and tamp well as you secure the bricks in place. Install the patio surface material. Tap the tops of the bricks with a rubber mallet and a short 2 × 4 to level them with one another (inset).

Concrete Curb Edging

Poured concrete edging is perfect for curves and custom shapes, especially when you want a continuous border at a consistent height. Keeping the edging low to the ground (about one inch above grade) makes it work well as a mowing strip, in addition to a patio or walkway border. Use fiber-reinforced concrete mix, and cut control joints into the edging to help control cracking.

Tools & Materials ▸

Rope or garden hose
Excavation tools
Mason's string
Hand tamp
Maul
Circular saw
Drill
Concrete
   mixing tools
Margin trowel
Wood concrete float

Concrete edger
1 × 1 wood stakes
¼" hardboard
1" wood screws
Fiber-reinforced
   concrete
Acrylic
   concrete sealer
Eye and
   ear protection
Work gloves

Concrete edging draws a sleek, smooth line between surfaces in your yard and is especially effective for curving paths and walkways.

How to Install Concrete Curb Edging

Lay out the contours of the edging using a rope or garden hose. For straight runs, use stakes and mason's string to mark the layout. Make the curb at least 5" wide.

Dig a trench between the layout lines 8" wide (or 3" wider than the finished curb width) at a depth that allows for a 4"-thick (minimum) curb at the desired height above grade. Compact the soil to form a flat, solid base.

Stake along the edges of the trench, using 1 × 1 × 12" wood stakes. Drive a stake every 18" along each side edge.

Build the form sides by fastening 4"-wide strips of ¼" hardboard to the insides of the stakes using 1" wood screws. Bend the strips to follow the desired contours.

Add spacers inside the form to maintain a consistent width. Cut the spacers from 1 × 1 to fit snugly inside the form. Set the spacers along the bottom edges of the form at 3-ft. intervals.

Fill the form with concrete mixed to a firm, workable consistency. Use a margin trowel to spread and consolidate the concrete.

Tool the concrete: once the bleed water disappears (see page 90), smooth the surface with a wood float. Using a margin trowel, cut 1"-deep control joints across the width of the curb at 3-ft. intervals. Tool the side edges of the curb with an edger. Allow to cure. Seal the concrete, as directed, with an acrylic concrete sealer, and let it cure for 3 to 5 days before removing the form.

Landscape Timber Edging

Pressure-treated landscape or cedar timbers make attractive, durable edging that's easy to install. Square-edged timbers are best for geometric pavers like brick and cut stone, while loose materials and natural flagstone look best with rounded or squared timbers. Choose the size of timber depending on how bold you want the border to look.

Tools & Materials ▸

Excavation tools
Plate compactor
  (available for rent)
Maul
Reciprocating saw
  with wood-cutting
  and metal-cutting
  blades, circular
  saw, or handsaw
Drill and ½" bit
Compacted gravel

Landscape fabric
Sand (optional)
Landscape timbers
  (pressure-treated
  or rot-resistant
  species only)
½"-diameter
  (#4) rebar
Eye and
  ear protection

Lumber or timber edging can be used with any patio surface material. Here, this lumber edging is not only decorative, it also holds all of the loose material in place.

How to Install Timber Edging

During the site excavation, dig a perimeter trench for the timbers so they will install flush with the top of the patio or walkway surface (or just above the surface for loose material). Add the compacted gravel base, as required, including a 2 to 4" layer in the perimeter trench. Cut timbers to the desired length using a reciprocating saw with a long wood-cutting blade, a circular saw, or a handsaw.

Drill ½" holes through each timber, close to the ends and every 24" in between. Cut a length of ½"-diameter (#4) rebar at 24" for each hole using a reciprocating saw and metal-cutting blade. Set the timbers in the trench and make sure they lie flat. Use your layout strings as guides for leveling and setting the height of the timbers. Anchor the timbers with the rebar, driving the bar flush with the wood surface.

Lumber Edging

Dimension lumber makes for an inexpensive edging material and a less-massive alternative to landscape timbers; 2 × 4 or 2 × 6 lumber works well for most patios and walkways. Use only pressure-treated lumber rated for ground contact or all-heart redwood or cedar boards to prevent rot. For the stakes, use pressure-treated lumber, since they will be buried anyway and appearance is not a concern.

Tools & Materials ▸

Excavation tools
Circular saw
Compactable gravel
Drill
2× lumber for edging
2 × 4 lumber for stakes
Wood preservative

Compacted gravel
Landscape fabric
Sand
2½" galvanized
   deck screws
Eye and ear
   protection

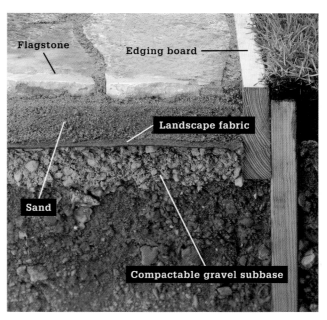

Wood edging is a popular choice for simple flagstone or paver walkways and for patios with a casual look.

How to Install Lumber Edging

Excavate the patio site, and dig a perimeter trench for the boards so they will install flush with the top of the patio surface (or just above the surface for loose material). Add the gravel base, as required, including a 2 to 4" layer of gravel in the trench. Cut the edging boards to length, and seal the ends with wood preservative. Cut 2 × 4 stakes about 16" long. Set the edging boards in the trench and drive a stake close to the ends of each board and every 24" in between.

Fasten the boards to the stakes with pairs of 2½" deck screws. Where boards meet at corners and butt joints, fasten them together with screws. Use your layout strings as guides for leveling and setting the height of the edging. Backfill behind the edging to support the boards and hide the stakes.

Low-voltage Landscape Lighting

Thanks to the many inexpensive and easy-to-install lighting kits and fixtures available, outdoor lighting has become a standard feature in today's home landscapes. A good lighting plan not only makes your patio and walkways more useful at night, it gives these spaces a second life with a completely different feel from the daytime setting.

Standard low-voltage lighting systems are commonly available in complete kits that include a low-voltage transformer, low-voltage cable, and several light fixtures, each with a wire lead that links to the main cable with a special connector. A basic landscape kit typically has three or more fixtures for standard in-ground installation. If you'd like to add specialty patio fixtures, such as step (or "brick") lights, pole- and wall-mount fixtures, and task lights for outdoor cooking, make sure your system is compatible with a full range of accessory lights. In addition to standard wired systems, you can find a wide variety of solar-powered fixtures that offer free operation and the easiest possible installation.

Here are some other factors to consider when choosing a standard low-voltage lighting system:

- **Transformer power**—For best performance, the total wattage of the light fixtures should be at least one-third of the transformer's wattage rating but should not exceed the wattage rating. If necessary, use two systems to avoid overloading a single system with too many fixtures.
- **Transformer controls**—Consider timers and photosensitive switches for automatic operation.
- **Cable gauge size**—12-gauge UF cable is recommended to reduce voltage drop in long cable runs.
- **Fixture and bulb brightness**—Brightness is often rated in foot-candles: one foot-candle is equivalent to the brightness of a 12-inch square area lit by a candle held 12 inches away. Use the brightness rating to guide the fixture layout.

As with indoor light fixtures, landscape lights can be just as beautiful as they are illuminating. Consider the look (and visibility) of fixtures in the daylight, in addition to their lighting characteristics at night.

Tools & Materials ▸

Drill and bits
Screwdrivers
Trenching spade
Low-voltage lighting kit
Paint stir-stick

PVC pipe
Hammer
Work gloves

Effective Lighting ▸

Here are some general design guidelines to keep in mind when planning your lighting scheme:

Keep it subtle. With the exception of surprise-oriented security lights (floodlights, motion detectors), outdoor lighting should be mellow and subdued—an intermingling of soft light and shadows, not a battle against the darkness.

Mix it up. The best lighting plans employ a combination of fixtures and levels of illumination. Use brighter or more direct lights to highlight a few landscape features or patio areas. Otherwise, stick to low, unobtrusive lighting. Variation helps emphasize key elements.

Illuminate surfaces, not people. Orient fixtures downward to light up paths and patio surfaces or upward for indirect background lighting. As a general rule, naked bulbs should be hidden from view. Never direct beams of light into a viewer's line of sight, which creates a harsh glare at night.

Use the right fixture for the job. There's an outdoor light for virtually every application. Some are decorative and made to be visible; others are easy to hide under low plantings or tuck away in the shadows.

Illuminate appropriately: Patios call for atmospheric lighting for nighttime use—so party guests can see one another (at least in dim light) and diners can see their food during evening meals. Provide a soft wash of background light with sconces mounted to the house wall or with post-fixtures with globes. For entertaining, a sprinkling of small accent lights along the patio's borders can create enough light for socializing while maintaining subtle ambiance.

Consider safety: Main traffic routes on and off a patio need lighting for safe and convenient travel. On patios, include lights at all changes in floor height and on any obstructions not clearly visible at night. Recessed lights on step risers provide a small amount of light precisely where it's needed. Paths are best lit with low-voltage pole fixtures; space fixtures 8 to 10 ft. apart for localized pools of light, or put them closer together to overlap their washes of light in a "spread" pattern.

Typical low-voltage outdoor lighting systems consist of: lens cap (A), lens cap posts (B), upper reflector (C), lens (D), base/stake/cable connector assembly (contains lower reflector) (E), low-voltage cable (F), lens hood (G), 7-watt 12-volt bulbs (H), cable connector caps (I), control box containing transformer and timer (J), and light sensor (K).

How to Install Low-Voltage Patio Lighting

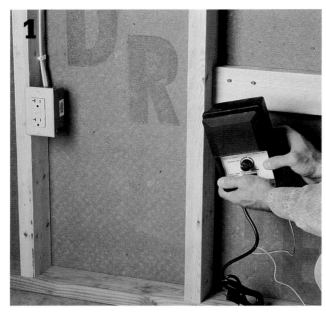

Determine where you will install the transformer(s)—either in the garage, on an exterior house wall, or on an outdoor post buried in the ground with concrete. If installing the transformer in the garage, mount it on a wall within 24" of a GFCI receptacle and at least 12" above the floor. See variation (below) for alternative installations.

Drill a hole through the wall or rim joist for the low-voltage cable and any sensors to pass through (inset). If a circuit begins in a high-traffic area, it's a good idea to protect the cable by running it through a short piece of PVC pipe or conduit and then into the shallow trench (see step 9).

Planning Tip ▸

Make a diagram of your yard and mark the location of new fixtures. Note the wattages of the fixtures and use the diagram to select a transformer and plan the circuits.

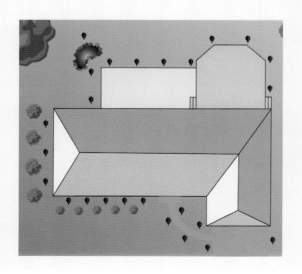

Variation: To install the transformer(s) to an outdoor wall or post, mount the unit within 24" of an outdoor GFCI receptacle and at least 12" above the ground. If the receptacle is exposed, install an "in-use" receptacle cover for added protection from the elements. Do not use an extension cord to connect the transformer.

3

Attach the end of the low-voltage wire to the terminals on the transformer. Make sure that both strands of wire are held tightly by their terminal screws.

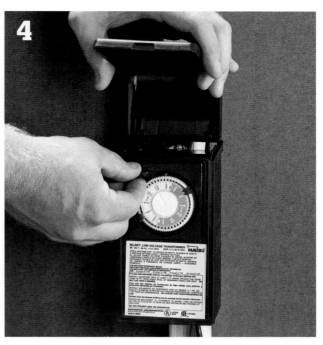

4

Transformers usually have a simple mechanism that allows you to set times for the lights to come on and go off automatically. Set these times before hanging the transformer.

5

Many low-voltage light fixtures are modular, consisting of a spiked base, a riser tube and a lamp. On these units, feed the wires and the wire connector from the light section down through the riser tube and into the base.

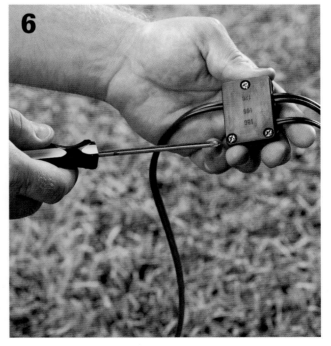

6

Take apart the connector box and insert the ends of the fixture wire and the low voltage landscape cable into it. Puncture the wire ends with the connector box leads. Reassemble the connector box. Feed the wire connector back into the light base and attach it according to directions that came with the lamp. In this model, all that was required was pushing the connector into a locking slot in the base.

(continued)

Install the low-voltage light bulb. Wrap the bulb with cloth to keep oil from your fingers off the glass.

After the bulb is installed, assemble the fixture parts that cover it, including the lens cap and reflector.

Lay out the lights, with the wires attached, in the pattern you have chosen. Then cut the sod between fixtures with a spade. Push the blade about 5" deep and pry open a seam by rocking the blade back and forth.

Gently force the cable into the slot formed by the spade; don't tear the wire insulation. A paint stick (or a cedar shingle) is a good tool for this job. Push the wire to the bottom of the slot.

Once the lamp is stabilized, tuck any extra wire into the slot using the paint stick. If you have a lot of extra wire, you can fold it and push the excess to the bottom of the slot. No part of the wire should be exposed when you are done with the job.

Firmly push the light into the slot in the sod. If the lamp doesn't seat properly, pull it out and cut another slot at a right angle to the first and try again.

Choosing Solar Landscape Lights ▸

Outdoor solar-powered lighting offers two distinct advantages over conventional low-voltage systems: easy, flexible installation and free power. Installing most landscape and patio light fixtures is as simple as staking the light into the ground or mounting it to a wall or post. Many fixtures, including path and accent lights, have a built-in solar panel, so the fixture can go anywhere it will be exposed to direct sunlight during the day. Brighter fixtures, like spot and security lights, often include a separate solar panel with a thin wire that delivers power to the light. The panel is mounted and positioned for maximum sun exposure, while the light fixture can be placed directly where it's needed. Most solar fixtures come with a photosensitive switch that automatically turns the light on at dusk and off at sunrise.

The main disadvantage of solar lighting is reliability. Lower quality fixtures and some high-power lights (such as spot lights) offer running times that won't last through the night. To minimize this problem, choose high-quality fixtures with advanced solar cells (better cells collect more power in low-light weather than cheaper cells) and efficient LED bulbs.

Solar landscape lights are available in sets and individual fixtures. You can pick and choose fixtures based on lighting needs as well as the fixtures' appearance and brightness. Best of all, you can easily reposition lights for desired effects throughout the seasons.

Landscaping with Plants

Plants are the eye-candy of a landscape, adding pops of color, ranges of texture, and intoxicating fragrances. This chapter contains a garden for every taste and the instructions you need to build them. If you live in an arid region or are increasingly concerned about water consumption, consider taking on our Xeriscape project that uses low-water use plants and hardscape. The Rain Garden project is an ecologically sound way of landscaping your yard. Meanwhile, we provide you with important nuts-and-bolts information that you'll use year-round, such as how to prune trees and properly mulch beds.

In this chapter:

- Gallery
- Planting Trees & Shrubs
- Tree Removal
- Pruning Trees & Shrubs
- Green Groundcover
- Mulching Beds
- Rain Garden
- Xeriscape

Gallery

Perennial plants tend to find their own order if you let them. As a general rule, allowing them to spread is a good strategy as long as they stay more or less within the confines you've created for them.

Dot your natural landscape with flowering perennials that are selected to bloom in succession throughout the growing season.

Plant ornamental grasses to provide rich colors and textures in any season.

Use garden pathways to direct foot traffic past your favorite landscape features, such as this reclined statue or the landscape bridge in the background.

Hedgerows and shrubberies define borders within your landscape. A dense row of hedges also adds some visual weight to a plain walkway and helps it succeed as a landscape feature.

Borders, perimeters and entrypoint markers require special attention so they stand out within your landscaped yard.

Use pots, window boxes and other planters to spruce up your yard and even add some whimsy.

A hint of a traditional formal garden is all it takes to make your ordinary landscape feel more studied and important. The island of greenery and Grecian-urn styled planter make a lovely highlight in a field of brick pavers.

Choose plants with interesting profiles and strong vertical presence to stand out in any landscape. Back-lighting from the front porch highlights the spiky shapes in this arid desertscape.

Planting Trees & Shrubs

Trees and shrubs are structural elements that provide many benefits to any property. Aside from adding structural interest to a landscape, they work hard to provide shade, block wind, and form walls and ceilings of outdoor living areas. Whether your landscape is a blank canvas or you plan to add trees and shrubs to enhance what's already there, you'll want to take great care when selecting what type of tree you plant, and how you plant it.

A substantially sized tree might be your greatest investment in plant stock, which is more reason to be sure you give that tree a healthy start by planting it correctly. Timing and transportation are the first issues you'll consider. The best time to plant is in spring or fall, when the soil is usually at maximum moistness and the temperature is moderate enough to allow roots to establish. When you choose a tree or shrub, protect the branches, foliage, and roots from wind and sun damage during transport. When loading and unloading, lift by the container or root ball, not the trunk. You may decide to pay a nursery to deliver specimens if they are too large for you to manage, or if you are concerned about damaging them en route to your property.

Tools & Materials ▸

Shovel	Long stake
Garden hose	Tree
Utility knife	Peat moss

Trees and shrubs are packaged three different ways for sale: with a bare root, container-grown, and balled-and-burlapped. Bare root specimens (left) are the most wallet-friendly, but you must plant them during the dormant season, before growing begins. Container-grown plants (center) are smaller and take years to achieve maturity, but you can plant them any time—preferably during spring or fall. Balled-and-burlapped specimens (right) are mature and immediately fill out a landscape. They are also the most expensive.

How to Plant a Balled-and-Burlapped Tree

Use a garden hose to mark the outline for a hole that is at least two or three times the diameter of the root ball. If you are planting trees with shallow, spreading roots (such as most evergreens) rather than a deep taproot, make the hole wider. Dig no deeper than the height of the rootball.

Amend some of the removed soil with hydrated peat moss and return the mixture to build up the sides of the hole, creating a medium that is easy for surface roots to establish in. If necessary (meaning, you dug too deep) add and compact soil at the bottom of the hole so the top of the rootball will be slightly above grade when placed.

Place the tree in the hole so the top of root ball is slightly above grade and the branches are oriented in a pleasing manner. Cut back the twine and burlap from around the trunk and let it fall back into the hole. Burlap may be left in the hole—it will degrade quickly. Non-degradable rootball wrappings should be removed.

Backfill amended soil around the rootball until the soil mixture crowns the hole slightly. Compress the soil lightly with your hands. Create a shallow well around the edge of the fresh soil to help prevent water from running off. Water deeply initially and continue watering very frequently for several weeks. Staking the tree is wise, but make sure the stake is not damaging the roots.

Tree Removal

Removing trees is often a necessary part of shaping a landscape. Diseased or dead trees need to be removed before they become a nuisance and to maintain the appearance of your landscape. Or, you may simply need to clear the area for any of a variety of reasons, including making a construction site, allowing sunshine to a planting bed, or opening up a sightline.

If you need to remove a mature tree from your yard, the best option is to have a licensed tree contractor cut it down and remove the debris. If you are ambitious and careful, small trees with a trunk diameter of less than six inches can present an opportunity for DIY treecutting. The first step in removing a tree is determining where you want it to fall. This area is called the felling path; you'll also need to plan for two retreat paths. Retreat paths allow you to avoid a tree falling in the wrong direction. To guide the tree along a felling path, a series of cuts are made in the trunk. The first cut, called a notch, is made by removing a triangle-shaped section on the side of the tree facing the felling path. A felling cut is then made on the opposite side, forming a wide hinge that guides the fall of the tree.

Always follow manufacturer's safety precautions when operating a chainsaw. The following sequence outlines the steps professionals use to fell a tree and cut it into sections. Always wear protective clothing, including gloves, hardhat, safety glasses, and hearing protection when felling or trimming trees. And make certain no children or pets are in the area.

Tools & Materials ▸

Chainsaw
Hard hat
Safety glasses
Ear protection
Wedge
Hand maul

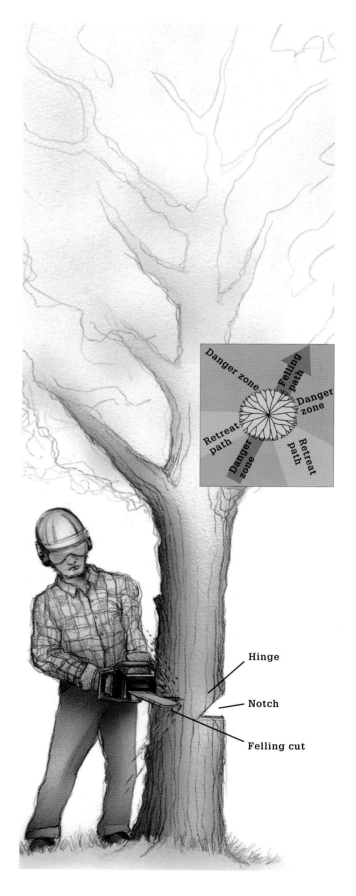

How to Fell a Tree

Remove limbs below head level. Start at the bottom of the branch, making a shallow up-cut. Then cut down from the top until the branch falls. *Note: Hire a tree service to cut down and remove trees with a trunk diameter of more than 6".*

Use a chain saw to make a notch cut one-third of the way through the tree, approximately at waist level. Do not cut to the center of the trunk. Make a straight felling cut about 2" above the base of the notch cut, on the opposite side of the trunk. Leave a 3"-thick "hinge" at the center.

Drive a wedge into the felling cut. Push the tree toward the felling path to start its fall, and move into a retreat path to avoid possible injury.

Standing on the opposite side of the trunk from the branch, remove each branch by cutting from the top of the saw, until the branch separates from the tree. Adopt a balanced stance, grasp the handles firmly with both hands, and be cautious with the saw.

To cut the trunk into sections, cut down two-thirds of the way and roll the trunk over. Finish the cut from the top, cutting down until the section breaks away.

Pruning Trees & Shrubs

Pruning trees and shrubs can inspire new growth and prolong the life of the plant. It may surprise you that the entire plant benefits when you remove select portions. Regular pruning also discourages disease and improves the plant's overall appearance.

Timing and technique when pruning will, quite literally, mold the future of the shrub or tree. The trick to properly pruning trees and shrubs is to remember that less is more. Instances that warrant pruning include: pinching off the ends of plants (to maintain a bushy look); restoring an ornamental's shape with clean-up cuts; and removing rubbing tree branches, where abrasion is an open wound for disease to enter.

Light, corrective pruning means removing less than 10 percent of the tree or shrub canopy. This can be performed at any time during the year. However, when making more severe cuts, such as heading back, thinning, or rejuvenating, prune when plants are under the least amount of stress. That way, trees and shrubs will have time to heal successfully before the flowering and growing season. The best time to perform heavy pruning/trimming on most woody plants, flower trees, and shrubs is during late winter and early spring.

Regular pruning of trees and shrubs not only keeps the plants looking neat and tidy, it makes them healthier.

Shrub Pruning ▸

Use a combination of these pruning methods to control shrub growth.

Pinching: The terminal of the shoot is the tip of the stem (green portion before it becomes woody). When you remove the terminal, the bud is lost allowing lateral buds to grow. Pinching reduces the length of a shoot and promotes side (filler) growth. Pinch off especially long shoots from inside the shrub canopy.

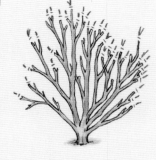

Heading back: Increase the density of a shrub by cutting terminal shoots back to a healthy branch or bud. Cut inward or outward growing shoots to manipulate the shape. Choose your growth direction, then remove buds accordingly. The top

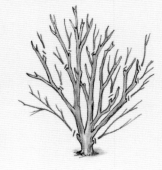

bud should be located on the side of the branch that faces the direction you want it to grow. For example, an inward-facing bud will develop into a branch that reaches into the canopy. If you allow two opposite-facing buds to grow, the result is a weak, Y-shaped branch.

Thinning: This involves cutting branches off the parent stem, so target the oldest, tallest stems first. (You'll need to reach into the shrub canopy to accomplish this successfully.) Prune branches that are one-third the diameter of the parent stem. To visualize where to cut, imagine the Y junction, where a lateral branch meets the parent stem. Practice moderation when thinning.

Rejuvenating: Remove the oldest branches by leaving little but a stub near the ground. Young branches can also be cut back, as well as thin stems.

Shearing: Swipe a hedge trimmer over the top of a shrub to remove the terminal of most shoots; this will give you a formal topiary look. Shear throughout the summer to maintain the shape. Keep in mind, shearing is more aesthetic than beneficial: it forces growth on the exterior of the plant, which blocks light and oxygen from the center. You're left with a shell of a shrub—leaves on the outside, naked branches on the inside.

Hedge Trimmers ▸

An electric or gas-powered hedge trimmer isn't just easier to use, it offers much greater control than pruning shears for shaping hedges during the pruning process.

Tree Pruning ▸

Always prune tree branches by cutting just outside the tree collar. You'll notice a circular closure around the wound as the tree begins to heal.

Thinning: These cuts reduce the tree canopy and allow wind to pass through branches. Thinning is a safety measure if you are concerned that a storm will damage a tree and surrounding property. Remove dead, broken, weak, and diseased branches. Cut them back to their point of origin or to laterals that are at least one-third the diameter of the branch you are removing. Be sure to remove less than 25 percent of foliage at one time. It's best to thin trees in the winter, when they are dormant.

Heading back: Reduce the size of your tree this way by cutting back lateral branches and then heating tips of laterals.

Reduction cut: Most common in younger trees, these cuts remove an offshoot branch back to a thicker branch attached to the tree trunk. Pictured below is a cut to remove a perpendicular branch.

How to Prune a Tree

Start by undercutting from beneath the limb with your bow saw or chain saw.

Finish the cut from above. This keeps the bark from tearing when the limb breaks loose.

Trim the stub from the limb so it's flush with the branch collar.

Green Groundcover

Groundcover is a practical solution for areas where grass won't grow, such as on slopes or in shady beds. It also adds texture and interest to a landscape and serves as a transition between planting areas. Ground cover refers to any vegetation that provides a dense, even cover. Most often, people think of ivy or low-growing pachysandra, but ground cover also includes evergreen and deciduous plants, herbaceous and woody species, ornamental grasses, perennials, and annuals. For example, planting carpet roses rather than ivy will provide a landscape bed with a fragrant swath of flowers.

By nature, ground covers spread, so it's important to think about how you'll control growth so it doesn't take over the landscape. Use edging at least four inches deep to contain creeping and spreading. Also, take care to properly prepare the soil. Start this project with loamy, well-balanced soil. Avoid planting ground cover in mid-summer, when hot sun adds stress to young plants. This project is best accomplished in early spring so root systems will develop before hot, dry months.

Dealing with Invasive Ivy ▶

Invasive ivy is like a rash that spreads—if you choose the wrong variety. The American Ivy Society selects an Ivy of the Year annually, and each cultivar is easy to grow, hardy, lush, beautiful, and not invasive in the garden. Try growing one of these suggested types of ivies:

- Lady Frances, Hedera helix
- Teardrop, Hedera helix
- Golden Ingot, Hedera helix
- Duck Foot, Hedera helix
- Misty, Hedera helix
- Anita, Hedera helix
- Shamrock, Hedera helix

For more information on invasive ivies, visit www.ivy.org.

Groundcover is created by low, sprawling perennials that require virtually no maintenance. Some examples include verbana (above), vinca and some varieties of ivy.

How to Establish Groundcover

Prepare the soil by breaking it up with hoe or cultivator and working it to a depth of 8" to 10". Incorporate a layer of organic matter, such as peat moss or compost. If soil is compacted, add peat moss or compost to improve porosity. Smooth the planting area with a rake until level.

Lay out plants in a staggered grid pattern. Refer to the informational stake from the nursery for watering and sunlight recommendations, as well as guidance on how close together plants should be placed. While the area might look sparse at first, groundcover plants will fill in and mature rapidly.

Dig a hole for each plant, using a hand trowel. Remove the plant from the pot and set it in the hole, gently pressing down roots so they make contact with soil. Repeat this process for each plant. Backfill over the top of the plant hole as necessary.

Water the plants deeply. Ensure that the soil is constantly moist for at least the first week after planting. Do not over-water—you should not allow standing pools of water to form at the bases of plants. Spread a thin layer of mulch around young plants to prevent soil from losing moisture and protect against erosion.

Mulching Beds

Mulch is the dressing on a landscape bed, but its benefits run deeper than surface appeal. Mulch protects plant and tree roots, prevents soil erosion, discourages weed growth, and helps the ground retain moisture. You can purchase a variety of mulches for different purposes. Synthetic mulches and stones are long-lasting, colorful, and resist erosion. They'll never break down. Organic mulches, such as compost and wood chips, enrich soil and double as "dressing" and healthy soil amendments.

No matter what type of mulch you choose, application technique is critical. If you spread it too thick it may become matted down and can trap too much moisture. Too thin, it can wash away to reveal bare spots. If it is unevenly applied it will appear spotty.

Consider timing before you apply mulch. The best time to mulch is mid- to late-spring, after the ground warms up. If you apply mulch too soon, the ground will take longer to warm up and your plants will suffer for it. You may add more mulch during the summer to retain water, and in the winter to insulate soil. (As weather warms, lift some of the mulch to allow new growth to sprout.) Spring is prime mulching time.

Mulches ▸

Organic:
- Compost
- Lawn clippings (free of chemicals)
- Leaves
- Wood chips or shavings
- Bark
- Manure

Synthetic and Stone:
- Recycled rubber mulch
- Stone or brick
- Landscape fabric

Mulch comes in many varieties, but most is made from shredded wood and bark. Because it is an organic material it breaks down and requires regular refreshing.

How to Landscape with Mulch

Remove weeds from the bed and water plants thoroughly before applying mulch. For ornamental plating beds it often is a good idea to lay strips of landscape fabric over the soil before mulching.

Option: Help contain the mulch in a confined area by installing flexible landscape edging.

Working in sections, scoop a pile of material from the load (wheelbarrow or bag) and place the piles around the landscape bed.

Spread mulch material to a uniform 1" thickness to start. Do not allow mulch to touch tree trunks or stems of woody ornamentals. Compost can double as mulch and a soil amendment that provides soil with nutrients. If you don't make your own compost, you can purchase all-natural products such as Sweet Peet.

Rain Garden

A rain garden collects and filters water runoff, which prevents flooding and protects the environment from pollutants carried by urban stormwater. Rain gardens provide a valuable habitat for birds and wildlife, and these purposeful landscape features also enhance the appearance of your yard. In fact, when a rain garden is installed and planted properly, it looks like any other landscape bed on a property. (There are no ponds or puddles involved.) The difference is, a rain garden can allow about 30 percent more water to soak into the ground than a conventional lawn.

Though a rain garden may seem like a small environmental contribution toward a mammoth effort to clean up our water supply and preserve aquifers, collectively they can produce significant community benefits. For instance, if homeowners in a subdivision each decide to build a rain garden, the neighborhood could avoid installing an unsightly retention pond to collect stormwater run-off. So you see, the little steps you take at home can make a big difference.

Most of the work of building a rain garden is planning and digging. If you recruit some helpers for the manual labor, you can easily accomplish this project in a weekend. As for the planning, give yourself good time to establish a well-thought-out design that considers the variables mentioned here. And as always, before breaking ground, you should contact your local utility company or digging hotline to be sure your site is safe.

Tools & Materials ▶

Shovels
Rakes
Trowels

Carpenter's level
Small backhoe
  (optional)

Tape measure
Wood stakes, at least
  2 ft. long

String
6 ft. 2 × 4 board
  (optional)

Before You Dig ▶

Determine the best place for your rain garden by answering the following questions:

- Where does water stand after a heavy rain?
- What is the water source? (drainpipe, run-off from a patio or other flat surface, etc.)
- What direction does water move on your property?
- Where could water potentially enter and exit a rain garden?
- Where could a rain garden be placed to catch water from its source before it flows to the lowest point on the property?
- Do you need more than one rain garden?

Preparing the Land

Soil is a key factor in the success of your rain garden because it acts as a sponge to soak up water that would otherwise run off and contribute to flooding, or cause puddling in a landscape. Soil is either sandy, silty, or clay-based, so check your yard to determine what category describes your property. Sandy soil is ideal for drainage, while clay soils are sticky and clumpy. Water doesn't easily penetrate thick, compacted clay soils, so these soils need to be amended to aerate the soil body and give it a porous texture that's more welcoming to water run-off. Silty soils are smooth but not sticky and absorb water relatively well, though they also require amending. Really, no soil is perfect, so you can plan on boosting its rain garden potential with soil amendments. The ideal soil amendment is comprised of: washed sharp sand (50%); double-shredded hardwood mulch (15%); topsoil (30%); and peat moss (5%). Compost can be substituted for peat moss.

While planning your rain garden, give careful consideration to its position, depth, and shape. Build it at least 10 feet from the house, and not directly over a septic system. Avoid wet patches where infiltration is low. Shoot for areas with full or partial sun that will help dry up the land, and stay away from large trees. The flatter the ground, the better. Ideally, the slope should be less than a 12% grade.

Residential rain gardens can range from 100 to 300 square feet in size, and they can be much smaller, though you will have less of an opportunity to embellish the garden with a variety of plants. Rain gardens function well when shaped like a crescent, kidney, or teardrop. The slope of the area where you're installing the rain garden will determine how deep you need to dig. Ideally, dig four to eight inches deep. If the garden is too shallow, you'll need more square footage to capture the water run-off, or risk overflow. If the garden is too deep, water may collect and look like a pond. That's not the goal.

Finally, as you consider the ideal spot for your rain garden—and you may find that you need more than one—think about areas of your yard that you want to enhance with landscaping. Rain gardens are aesthetically pleasing, and you'll want to enjoy all the hard work you put into preparing the land and planting annuals and perennials.

How to Build a Rain Garden

Choose a site, size and shape for the raingarden, following the design standards outlined on the previous two pages. Use rope or a hose to outline the rain garden excavation area. Avoid trees and be sure to stay at least 10 ft. away from permanent structures. Try to choose one of the recommended shapes: crescent, kidney, or tear drop.

Dig around the perimeter of the rain garden and then excavate the central area to a depth of 4 to 8". Heap excavated soil around the garden edges to create a berm on the three sides that are not at the entry point. This allows the rain garden to hold water in during a storm.

Dig and fill sections of the raingarden that are lower, working to create a level foundation. Tamp the top of the berm so it will stand up to water flow. The berm eventually can be planted with grasses or covered with mulch.

Level the center of the rain garden and check with a long board with a carpenter's level on top. Fill in low areas with soil and dig out high areas. Move the board to different places to check the entire garden for level. *Note: If the terrain demands, a slope of up to 12% is okay. Then, rake the soil smooth.*

Plant specimens that are native to your region and have a well-established root system. Contact a local university extension or nursery to learn which plants can survive in a saturated environment (inside the rain garden). Group together bunches of 3 to 7 plants of like variety for visual impact. Mix plants of different heights, shapes, and textures to give the garden dimension. Mix sedges, rushes, and native grasses with flowering varieties. The plants and soil cleanse stormwater that runs into the garden, leaving pure water to soak slowly back into the earth.

Apply double-shredded mulch over the bed, avoiding crowns of new transplants. Mulching is not necessary after the second growing season. Complement the design with natural stone, a garden bench with a path leading to it, or an ornamental fence or garden wall. Water a newly established rain garden during drought times—as a general rule, plants need 1 in. of water per week. After plants are established, you should not have to water the garden. Maintenance requirements include minor weeding and cutting back dead or unruly plant material annually.

Xeriscape

Xeriscaping, in a nutshell, is waterwise gardening. It is a form of landscaping using drought-tolerant plants and grasses. How a property is designed, planted, and maintained can drastically reduce water usage if xeriscape is put into practice. Some think that xeriscaping will become a new standard in gardening as water becomes a more precious commodity and as homeowners' concern for the environment elevates.

Several misconceptions about xeriscaping still exist. Many people associate it with desert cactus and dirt, sparsely placed succulents and rocks. They are convinced that turf is a four-letter word and grass is far too thirsty for xeriscaping. This is not true. You can certainly include grass in a xeriscape plan, but the key is to incorporate turf where it makes the most sense: children's play areas or front yards protected from foot traffic. Also, your choice of plants expands far beyond prickly cactus. The plant list, depending on where you live, is long and varied.

Tools & Materials ▸

Basic tools   Fill

Xeriscaping is associated with sand, cacti, and arid climates, but the basic idea of planting flora that withstands dry conditions and makes few demands on water resources is a valid goal in any area.

The Seven Principles of Xeriscape

Keep in mind these foundation principles of Xeriscape as you plan a landscape design. First begin by finding out what the annual rainfall is in your area. What time of year does it usually rain? Answering these questions will help guide plant selection. Now look at the micro-environment: your property. Where are there spots of sun and shade? Are there places where water naturally collects and the ground is boggy? What about dry spots where plant life can't survive? Where are trees, structures (your home), patios, walkways, and play areas placed? Sketch your property and figure these variables into your Xeriscape design.

Also, carefully study these seven principles and work them into your plan.

1. **Water conservation:** Group plants with similar watering needs together for the most efficient water use. Incorporate larger plantings that provide natural heating and cooling opportunities for adjacent buildings. If erosion is a problem, build terraces to control water runoff. Before making any decision, ask yourself: How will this impact water consumption?

2. **Soil improvement:** By increasing organic matter in your soil and keeping it well aerated, you provide a hardy growing environment for plants, reducing the need for excess watering. Aim for soil that drains well and maintains moisture effectively. Find out your soil pH level by sending a sample away to a university extension or purchasing a home kit. This way, you can properly amend soil that is too acidic or alkaline.

3. **Limited turf areas:** Grass isn't a no-no, but planting green acres with no purpose is a waste. The typical American lawn is not water-friendly—just think how many people struggle to keep their lawns green during hot summers. If you choose turf, ask a nursery for water-saving species adapted to your area.

4. **Appropriate plants:** Native plants take less work and less water to thrive. In general, drought-resistant plants have leaves that are small, thick, glossy, silver-grey, or fuzzy. These attributes help plants retain water. As a rule, hot, dry areas with south and west exposure like drought-tolerant plants; while north- and east-facing slopes and walls provide moisture for plants that need a drink more regularly. Always consider a plant's water requirements and place those with similar needs together.

5. **Mulch:** Soil maintains moisture more effectively when its surface is covered with mulch such as leaves, coarse compost, pine needles, wood chips, bark, or gravel. Mulch will prevent weed growth and reduce watering needs when it is spread three inches thick.

6. **Smart irrigation:** If you must irrigate, use soaker hoses or drip irrigation (see page 112). These systems deposit water directly at plants' roots, minimizing run-off and waste. The best time to water is early morning.

7. **Maintenance:** Sorry, there's no such thing as a no-maintenance lawn. But you can drastically cut your outdoor labor hours with Xeriscape. Just stick to these principles and consider these additional tips: 1) plant windbreaks to keep soil from drying out (see page 52); 2) if possible, install mature plants that require less water than young ones; 3) try "cycle" irrigation where you water to the point of seeing run-off, then pause so the soil can soak up the moisture before beginning to water again.

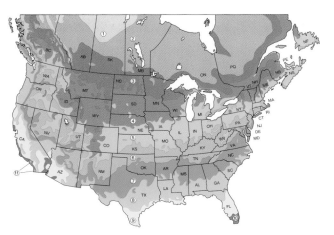

**RANGE OF
AVERAGE ANNUAL
MINIMUM TEMPERATURES
FOR EACH ZONE**

ZONE 1: BELOW -50∞F
ZONE 2: -50 TO -40∞F
ZONE 3: -40 TO -30∞F
ZONE 4: -30 TO -20∞F
ZONE 5: -20 TO -10∞F
ZONE 6: -10 TO 0∞F
ZONE 7: 0 TO 10∞F
ZONE 8: 10 TO 20∞F
ZONE 9: 20 TO 30∞F
ZONE 10: 30 TO 40∞F
ZONE 11: 40 TO 50∞F

How to Xeriscape Your Yard

Plan the landscape with minimal turf, grouping together plants with similar water requirements. Refer to the Seven Principles of Xeriscape as you sketch. Always consider your region's climate, and your property's microclimate: rainfall, sunny areas, shady spots, wind exposure, slopes (causing run-off), and high foot-traffic zones.

Divide your Xeriscape landscape plan into three zones. The oasis is closest to a large structure (your home) and can benefit from rain runoff and shade. The transition areas is a buffer between the oasis and arid zones. Arid zones are farthest away from structures and get the most sunlight. These conditions will dictate the native plants you choose.

Plant in receding layers by installing focal-point plants closest to the home (or any other structure), choosing species that are native to the area. As you get farther away from the home, plant more subtle varieties that are more drought-tolerant.

As you plant beds, be sure to group together plants that require more water so you can efficiently water these spaces.

5

Incorporate groundcover on slopes, narrow strips that are difficult to irrigate and mow, and shady areas where turf does not thrive. Install hardscape such as walkways, patios, and stepping-stone paths in high foot-traffic zones.

6

Mulch will help retain moisture, reduce erosion, and serves as a pesticide-free weed control. Use it to protect plant beds and fill in areas where turf will not grow.

7

Plant turf sparingly in areas that are easy to maintain and will not require extra watering. Choose low-water use grasses adapted for your region. These may include Kentucky Bluegrass, Zoysia, St. Augustine, and Buffalo grass.

Option: Install a drip irrigation system to water plants efficiently.

Landscaping with Water

Water is a key element in any landscape, working both as a decorative element and as a critical part of the ecosystem. Moving water can set a mood for all the senses, as its gurgling sounds can lull you into a peaceful state of mind (and also deaden outside noise that is less desirable). A garden pond serves as a focal point and allows you to introduce whole new classes of plantlife, including floating plants such as water lilies and marginal species such as cattails. Whether it resides in a pond, a stream, a classical fountain or even a waterfall, water will transform your landscape.

Along with its aesthetic benefits, water must be delivered to the living matter throughout your yard. For large yards where watering by hand or with sprinklers can be very time consuming, water delivery can be done through very practical means like drip irrigation or automatic, in-ground irrigation systems. And installing a rain barrel or two is a convenient way to keep a ready supply of free water near your house, garage, or shed.

In this chapter:

- Gallery
- Rain Barrel
- Drip Irrigation
- In-ground Sprinkler System
- Hard-shell Pond & Fountain
- Freeform Garden Pond

Gallery

This complex backyard waterfall splits in two directions, making it a more challenging project to build. Your friends and neighbors will appreciate the effort.

A well-planned sprinkler system delivers water to thirsty landscape beds and turf.

Cascading water pots fashioned from exposed aggregate concrete have a significant calming effect while occupying only a small amount of real estate.

Local flagstone is stacked to form a dramatic fountain structure in the center of this fieldstone-lined garden pond.

Larger specimen rocks create a pond border and line the streambed in this backyard water feature. The shallow pool at the end of the waterfall is a perfect spot for goldfish.

Capture stormwater and runoff with a rain barrel. A traditional coopered oak barrel is always desirable if you find one.

A touch of Tuscany reveals itself in this classical garden pool and surroundings.

Concrete is formed and poured in place to create this custom waterfall concourse.

Rain Barrel

One of the simplest, least expensive ways to irrigate a landscape is with a system that collects and stores rainwater for controlled distribution either through a garden hose or a drip irrigation system.

The most common system includes one or more rain barrels (typically 40 to 80 gallons in capacity) connected to downspouts. Valve fittings at the bottoms of the barrels let you connect them to a hose or to a drip irrigation line. The system can be configured as a primary irrigation system or a secondary system to augment a standard irrigation system.

Some communities now offer subsidies for rain barrel use, offering free or reduced-price barrels and downspout connection kits. Check with your local water authorities.

Tools & Materials ▸

Drill	Downspout diverter
Hacksaw	(optional)
Rain barrel kit	Pavers or blocks (optional)

How to Install a Rain Barrel System

Select a location for the barrel under a downspout. Locate your barrel as close to the area you want to irrigate as possible. Make sure the barrel has a stable, level base. Connect the overflow tube, and make sure it is pointed away from the foundation.

Connect the spigot near the bottom of the barrel. Some kits may include a second spigot for filling watering cans. Use Teflon tape at all threaded fittings to ensure a tight seal. Remove the downspout, and set the barrel on its base.

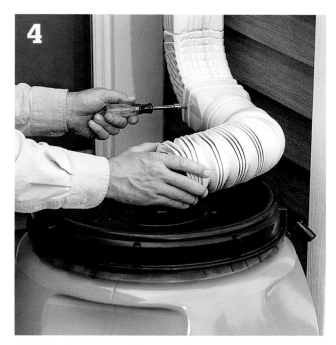

Cut the downspout to length with a hacksaw. Reconnect the elbow fitting to the downspout using sheet metal screws. Attach the cover to the top of the rain barrel. Some systems include a cover with porous wire mesh, to which the downspout delivers water. Others include a cover with a sealed connection (next step).

Link the downspout elbow to the rain barrel with a length of flexible downspout extension attached to the elbow and the barrel cover.

Variation: If your barrel comes with a downspout adapter, cut away a segment of downspout and insert the adapter so it diverts water into the barrel.

Connect a drip irrigation tube or garden hose to the spigot. A Y-fitting, like the one shown here, will let you feed the drip irrigation system through a garden hose when the rain barrel is empty.

If you want, increase water storage by connecting two or more rain barrels together with a linking kit, available from many kit suppliers.

Drip Irrigation

Plants love deep, long drinks of water, and this can best be accomplished through water-saving drip irrigation. Rather than dousing plant beds with a hit of water, which can pool on the surface and run off rather than sinking down to feed roots, drip irrigation's misty spray or gurgling drip (depending on the system) take time to feed plants slowly. Not a drop of water is wasted, making this method the most "green" way to water plant beds that require such maintenance.

Tools & Materials ▸

Drip irrigation kit
Tubing punch

Extra fittings,
    as needed

Drip irrigation systems offer many different types of fittings, including the spray head shown here. Because they precisely direct water exactly where it's needed, drip systems waste very little water. A thick layer of mulch around plants will help keep soil moist.

Irrigation Equipment

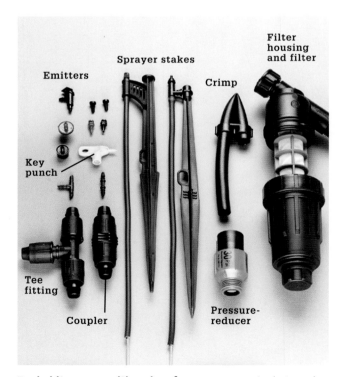

Emitters

Sprayer stakes

Filter housing and filter

Crimp

Key punch

Tee fitting

Coupler

Pressure-reducer

Basic kits come with only a few components, but can be augmented with pieces purchased "a la carte." You'll also need a punch for piercing the tubing and "goof plugs" for repairing errant punches.

Tubing for drip irrigation is thin-wall flexible polyethylene or polyvinyl, typically ¼" or ½" in diameter. Internal diameters can vary from manufacturer to manufacturer, so it's a good idea to purchase pipe and fittings from a single source.

How to Install a Drip Irrigation System

Connect the system's supply tube to a water source, such as a hose spigot or a rainwater system. If you tap into your household water supply, use a pressure gauge to check water pressure. If pressure exceeds 50 pounds per square inch (psi), install a pressure-reducing fitting before attaching the feeder tube. A filter should also be attached to the faucet before the feeder tube.

At garden bed locations, begin installing drip emitters every 18". You can also purchase ½" PE tubing with emitters preinstalled. If you use this tubing, cut the feeder tube once it reaches the first bed, and attach the emitter tubing with a barbed coupling. Route the tubing among the plants so that emitters are over the roots.

For trees and shrubs, make a branch loop around the tree. Pierce the feed tube near the tree and insert a T-fitting. Loop the branch around the tree and connect it to both outlets on the T-fitting. Use ¼" tubing for small trees, ½" for larger specimens. Insert emitters in the loop every 18".

Use micro sprayers for hard-to-reach plants. Sprayers can be connected directly to the main feeder line or positioned on short branch lines. Sprayers come in a variety of spray patterns and flow rates; choose one most appropriate for the plants to be watered.

Potted plants and raised beds can also be watered with sprayers. Place stake-mounted sprayers in the pots or beds. Connect a length of ¼" tubing to the feeder line with a coupler, and connect the ¼" line to the sprayer.

Once all branch lines and emitters are installed, flush the system by turning on the water and let it flow for a full minute. Then, close the ends of the feeder line and the branch lines with figure-8 end crimps. Tubing can be left exposed or buried under mulch.

EcoTip ▶

For a fast drip irrigation solution, use a soaker hose with tiny holes. You can snake the hose through a landscape bed or bury it under mulch. Cut the hose to a desired length and use end caps or hose fittings, as needed. These hoses have a 2- to 3-inch watering width.

In-ground Sprinkler System

Sprinkler systems offer a carefree means of keeping your lawn and garden green. Home improvement centers and landscaping retailers sell kits as well as individual components for installing in-ground systems. Installing a system can take a bit of time, but it's not at all difficult. The most challenging part of the job might be tapping into your home's plumbing system. If you're unsure of your abilities here, you can install everything but the final hookups, then hire a plumber to tap into the plumbing system.

For larger yards, design a sprinkler system with several zones, each serviced by a separate feeder pipe. Water is distributed to these zones at a manifold connected to the main supply line.

Before beginning an irrigation system project, check with your local building department. You may need a permit. Also check local requirements regarding backflow prevention or antisiphon devices. Before you dig trenches, call your utility company to have any utility lines marked.

A variety of timers are available for automating any irrigation system. More expensive models will control as many as 16 different zones, and may have rain sensors that prevent the system from operating if it is raining. The instructions will vary depending on the type of timer and accessory you buy, but all operate in largely the same way: the timer plugs into an ordinary receptacle, and sends its control signals to the manifold valves through low-voltage wires.

Tools & Materials ▸

Bucket
Stopwatch
Pressure valve
Drill with 1" bit
Shovel
Utility knife
Compression T-fitting
PVC pipe
PVC valves & fittings
PVC solvent glue

Antisiphon fitting
Irrigation manifold
  with control module
  & controller
Wooden stakes & string
PVC or PE
  irrigation pipe
T-fittings & L-fittings
Irrigation risers
Irrigation heads

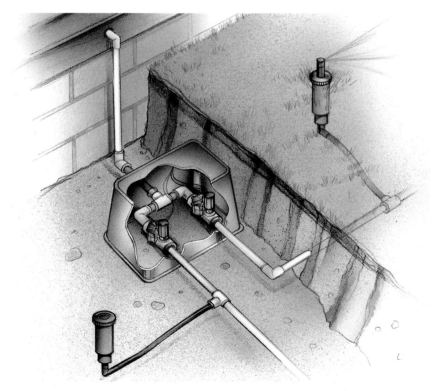

Water from the house supply (or sometimes an external source such as a river and pump) enters a manifold in the irrigation system and is apportioned out to a network of sprinkler heads from the manifold.

The manifold for a sprinkler system typically is buried in a shallow box in the yard and covered with an easily removed lid.

How to Design an In-ground Sprinkler System

To measure the flow rate of your water service, set a gallon bucket under an outdoor spigot. Open the faucet all the way and record the amount of time it takes to fill the bucket. To calculate the gallons per minute (GPM), divide 60 by the number of seconds it took to fill the gallon bucket. So, if it took 6 seconds, then 60/6 equals 10 GPM. This number will determine the size of your manifold and feeder pipe.

Now measure the pressure of your water system. Make sure all faucets in the house are off. Attach a pressure valve to any faucet in the system and open its valve all the way. Record the reading.

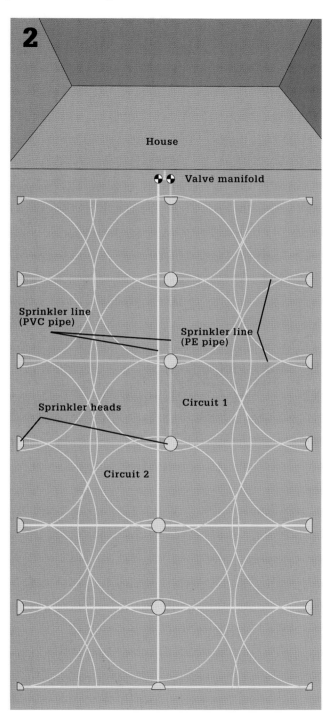

Make a sketch showing layout of spinkler heads. Follow manufacturer's instructions for overlapping head spray patterns. Keep heads at least 6" from sidewalks, driveways, and buildings. Next, mark the irrigation manifold location and create zones for your sprinkler heads. Locate the manifold near the water meter. Zones are individual runs of PVC or PE supply pipe the same size as your water main. Turns and changes of elevation can reduce efficiency, so try to design zones with few turns or rises.

How to Install a Sprinkler System

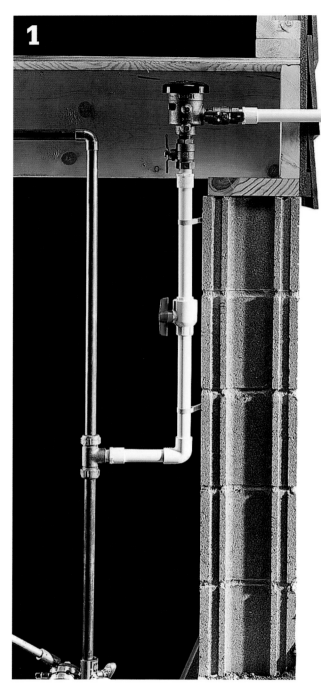

1

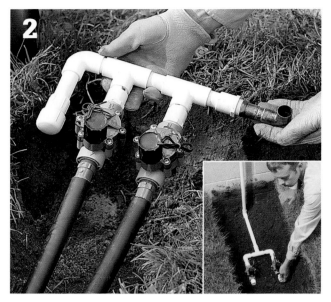

2

Choose a manifold with as many outlets as you have zones. The manifold shown here has two zones. Assemble the manifold as directed (some come preassembled, others are solvent-glued) and set it in the hole. Connect the supply pipe from the house to the manifold with an automated control module. install the controller on the house near the supply pipe (inset) and run the included wires under the supply pipe from the valves to control module.

3

Tap into your water supply. Shut off the water at the main shutoff valve. On the downstream side of your water meter, install a compression T-fitting. To supply the irrigation system, you will need to run PVC pipe to the manifold location. At a convenient location inside the house, install a gate valve with bleed in the line. Outside, dig a 10" trench leading to the manifold location. Drill a 1" hole through the sill directly above the trench, and route the pipe through the hole and down to the trench, using an L-fitting. You may also need to install a backflow prevention or an antisiphon device between the main and the irrigation manifold; check local code.

Mark the sprinkler locations. Use stakes or landscape flags to mark the sprinkler locations and then mark the pipe routes with spray paint or string. Once all the locations are marked, dig the trenches. In nonfreezing climates, trenches can be as little as 6". In freezing climates, dig trenches at least 10" deep. Renting a trencher can speed the job considerably. Set the sod aside so you can replace it after the sprinklers are installed.

Lay the pipe. Work on one zone at a time, beginning at the manifold. Connect the first section of PVC or PE pipe (PE shown) to the manifold outlet with solvent glue for PVC, or a barbed coupler and pipe clamps for PE (shown). At the first sprinkler location, connect a T-fitting with a female-threaded outlet for the riser. Continue with the next run of PE to the next sprinkler location. Install T-fittings at each sprinkler location. At the end of each zone, install an L-fitting for the last sprinkler.

Install the risers for the sprinkler heads. Risers come in a variety of styles. The simplest are short, threaded pipe nipples, but flexible and cut-to-fit risers are also available. Use a riser recommended by the manufacturer for your sprinkler head. For pop-up heads, make sure the nipple is the correct length for proper sprinkler operation.

Once all the risers are in place, flush the system. Turn on the water and open the valves for each zone one at a time, allowing the water to run for about a minute or until it runs clear. After the system is flushed, begin installing the sprinkler heads. Thread the heads onto the risers and secure them in place with earth. Make sure the heads are vertical (stake the risers if necessary). Fill in the rest of the trenches and replace the sod.

Variation: In freezing climates, it's a good idea to install a valve with a fitting that allows the system to be drained with compressed air. Install the fitting downstream of any antisiphon valves but before the manifold. In the fall, close the irrigation system's shutoff valve and open any drain valves. At the manifold, open one zone's valve and blow air into the zone until no water comes out. Repeat for each zone.

Hard-shell Pond & Fountain

A small pond and fountain add more than the illusion of luxury to landscapes; they also add the sound and sparkle of moving water and invite birds to join the party. Installing a pond and fountain can be heavy work, but it's not at all complicated. If you can use a shovel and read a level, you can install a beautiful fountain like the classic Roman fountain shown here.

Most freestanding fountains are designed to be set into an independently installed water feature. The fountains typically are preplumbed with an integral pump, but larger ones may have an external pumping apparatus. The kind of kit you'll find at your local building or garden center normally comes in at least two parts: the pedestal and the vessel.

The project shown here falls into the luxury-you-can-afford category and is fully achievable for a DIYer. If the project you have in mind is of massive scale (with a pond larger than around 8 × 10 ft.) you'll likely need to work with a pondscaping professional to acquire and install the materials needed for such an endeavor.

You can install a fountain in an existing water feature, or you can build a new one with a hard liner, as shown here, or with a soft liner (see pages 124 to 127). Have your utility providers mark the locations of all utility lines before beginning this or any project that involves digging.

Tools & Materials ▸

Level	Interlocking
Shovel or spade	paving stones
Hand tamp	Rubber floor mat
Rope	Freestanding
Preformed	fountain
pond liner	Fountain pedestal
Sand	Tarp
Compactable gravel	River stones

The work necessary to install a garden pond and fountain will pay dividends for many years to come. The process is not complicated, but does involve some fairly heavy labor, such as digging and hauling stones.

Installing Ponds & Fountains

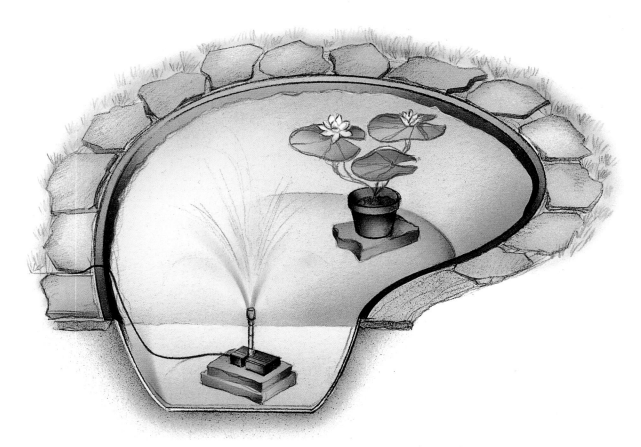

A hard shell-type liner combines well with a fountain because its flat, hard bottom makes a stable surface for resting the fountain base. You may need to prop up the fountain to get it to the optimal level.

If you plan to stock your pond with plant life or livestock, it's important to keep a healthy balance. For stocking with fish, the pond must be at least 24" deep, and you should have at least one submerged water plant to create oxygen.

How to Install a Pond & Fountain

Choose a flat area of your yard. Set the hard-shell pond liner right-side up in the installation area and adjust it until you are pleased with the location (it should be well away from buried utility lines). Hold a level against the edge of the top of the liner and use it as a guide to transfer the liner shape onto the ground below with a rope.

Cut away the sod within the outline. Measure the liner at the center and excavate the base area to this depth. Dig the hole 2 to 3" deeper than the liner, and dig past the outline a couple of inches all the way around. If the sides of your liner are sloped, slope the edges of the hole to match.

Remove any rocks or debris on the bottom of the hole, and add sand to cover the bottom of the hole about 2" deep. Test fit the liner and adjust the sand until the underside of the liner rim is slightly above ground and the liner is level from side to side.

Cut away the sod beyond the liner excavation area and dig out an area wide enough to accommodate your paving stones (called coping stones), about 1" deeper than the average stone thickness. Flagstone is the most common natural stone choice for coping because it is flat; concrete pavers also may be used easily. Make sure the surface of the excavation is as level as possible.

5

Fill the liner with 4 to 6" of water. Fill the space between the liner and the sides of the hole with damp sand, using a 2 × 4 to tamp it down as you go. Add more water and then more sand; continue until the pond and the gap are filled.

6

Bail about half of the water out of the pond. Place an exterior-rated rubber floor mat (or mats) at least ½" thick on the liner in the spot where you'd like the fountain to rest.

7

Feed the fountain's power cord up through the access holes in the pedestal. Set the fountain in place on top of the pedestal and run the cord to the edge.

8

Check to make sure the pedestal is level. If necessary, shim the pedestal with small flat stones to make the fountain level.

(continued)

Cover the pond and pedestal with a clean tarp, and add an inch of compactable gravel to the excavated area for the paving stones. Tamp down the gravel and check the area with a level. Cut a small channel for the power cord and route it beyond the excavated area toward a power source.

Set interlocking pavers in place around the lip of the liner. Adjust compactable gravel as necessary to make the pavers level. Add 1 to 3" of water to stabilize the liner.

Ponds look more natural if you line the bottoms with rock. Small-diameter (2 to 3") river rock is a good choice. Before putting it into the pond, rinse the rock well. One trick is to put the nozzle of a hose in the bottom of a clean 5-gallon bucket and then fill the bucket with dirty rock. Turn on the hose and let the water run for 15 minutes or so. This will cause impurities to float up and out of the bucket.

Cover the bottom of the liner with washed river rock. Place the fountain onto the pedestal and submerge the cord, running it out of the pond in an inconspicuous spot, such as between two pavers.

Completely fill both the pond and the fountain's base with water. If you will not be stocking the pond with fish or plants, add two ounces of chlorine bleach for every 10 gallons of water.

Allow the water to settle for 30 minutes or so, and then turn on the fountain pump and test. Let the pump run for an hour or so, and then turn it off and remove the fountain head. Use a hose and spray nozzle to clear out any blockages. Perform this maintenance regularly and whenever you notice that the spray from the fountain seems to be restricted.

Power Cord Management ▶

There are many ways to provide electrical power to operate the fountain pump. The best way is to add a new outdoor circuit, but this requires an electrician if you are not experienced with home wiring. The easier route is to feed your fountain pump with an exterior-rated extension cord that's plugged into an existing outdoor receptacle. Because having an extension cord laying in your lawn is both a tripping hazard and an electrical hazard (lawn mowers and wiring do not get along), you can bury the cord in a shallow trench. To protect it from digging instruments, either backfill with rocks so you know the exact location of the cord, or bury it encased in heavy conduit.

Avoid using this tactic if the pond is located more than 50 feet from the power source.

Dig a trench about 6" deep and 6" wide from the pond to your outdoor power source.

Feed the cord through conduit and lay the conduit in the trench all the way from the pond to the power source. Backfill the trench with dirt.

Freeform Garden Pond

A tranquil reflecting pond serves as a focal point in an outdoor room and a fertile setting for water-loving plants. A pond's shape can take on any configuration if you use soft, pliable pond liner. Once complete, your pond will become an anchor for additional landscape elements, such as a bridge, or stonescaping by placing appealing natural rock as a border.

EDPM (ethylene propylene diene monomer) liners are made from a synthetic rubber that is highly flexible, extremely durable, and fish-friendly. EDPM liners remain flexible at temperatures ranging from -40 to 175° Fahrenheit. These are cost-effective and easy to find at building or garden centers or landscape supply stores. Look for a liner that is 45 mil thick. Some landscape supply centers carry pond liner by the lineal foot.

Tools & Materials ▸

Level
Shovel or spade
Hand tamp
Tape measure
Garden hose or rope
Spray paint
Pond underlayment
Flexible pond liner
Sand
Compactable gravel
Flagstone pavers

River rocks
Plants (optional)
Fish (optional)

Free-form ponds blend into the landscape, especially with the addition of coping stones set into the edges. Building one involves heavy labor, but no special skills.

How to Create a Freeform Garden Pond

Sizing Your Liner ▶

Flexible liners adapt to nearly any shape or size pond you want. They can fit a typical kidney-shaped excavation with planting shelves, like the one shown here, or a very unique shape of your own design. EPDM rubber liner material is sold in precut sizes at your local home and garden center.

Select a location well away from buried utility lines. Use a garden hose or a rope to outline the pond. Avoid very sharp turns, and try for a natural looking configuration. When you're satisfied with the pond's shape, lift the hose or rope and use spray paint to mark the perimeter.

Find the lowest point on the perimeter and flag it for reference as the elevation benchmark. This represents the top of the pond's water-holding capacity, so all depth measurements should be taken from this point. Start digging at the deepest point (usually the middle of the pond) and work out toward the edges. For border plantings, establish one 6- to 8"-wide ledge about 12" down from the benchmark.

Set a level on the plant shelf to confirm that it is the same elevation throughout. Unless your building site is perfectly level or you have done a lot of earth moving, the edges of the pond are not likely to be at the same elevation, so there may be some pond liner visible between the benchmark and the high point. This can usually be concealed with plants, rocks, or by overhanging your coping more in high areas.

(continued)

Dig a 4"-deep by 12"-wide frame around the top of the hole to make room for the coping stones (adjust the width if you are using larger stones). Remove any rocks, debris, roots, or anything sharp in the hole, and add a 2" layer of sand to cover the bottom of the frame.

Cover the bottom and sides of the excavation with pond underlayment. Pond underlayment is a shock-absorbing, woven fabric that you should be able to buy from the same source that provides your liner. If necessary, cut triangles of underlayment and fit them together, overlapping pieces as necessary to cover the contours. This is not a waterproof layer.

Lay out the liner material and let it warm in the sun for an hour or two. Arrange the liner to cover the excavation, folding and overlapping as necessary. Place rocks around the edges to keep it from sliding into the hole.

Begin filling the pond with water. Watch the liner as the water level gets higher, and adjust and tuck it to minimize sharp folds and empty pockets.

Add some larger stones to the pond as the water rises, including a flat stone for your pond pump/filter. If the pump/filter has a fountain feature, locate it near the center. If not, locate it near the edge in an easy-to-reach spot.

Fill the pond all the way to the top until it overflows at the benchmark. Remove the stones holding the liner in place and begin laying flat stones, such as flagstones, around the perimeter of the pond. Cut and trim flagstones as necessary to minimize gaps.

Finish laying the coping stones and fill in gaps with cutoff and shards. If you are in a temperate climate, consider mortaring the coping stones, but be very careful to keep wet mortar out of the water: it kills plants and damages pump/filters. Set flagstone pavers on the ledge at the perimeter of the pond. Add more water and adjust the liner again. Fill the pond to just below the flagstones, and trim the liner.

Consult a garden center, an extension agent from a local university, or the Internet to help you choose plants for your pond. Include a mixture of deep-water plants, marginals, oxygenators, and floating plants. Place the plants in the pond. If necessary to bring them to the right height, set the plants on bricks or flat stones. Spread decorative gravel, sand, or mulch to cover the liner at the perimeter of the pond. Install plants along the pond's margins, if desired.

Landscaping with Stone

tone in its many forms adds character to a landscape—a sense of earthen timelessness that feels like it has been on the property forever and that it belongs there, no matter how new the project is. With the array of convincing manufactured pavers on the market that look like the "real thing," creating a stone patio or retaining wall is much easier for the homeowner to accomplish. In this chapter, we provide a collection of projects using natural and manufactured stone pavers.

In this chapter:

- Gallery
- Interlocking Block Retaining Wall
- Stone Retaining Wall
- Drystack Stone Wall
- Mortared Stone Wall
- Repairing a Stone Wall
- Loose Rock Landscape Path
- Stepping Stone Landscape Path
- Timber & Gravel Landscape Steps
- Flagstone Landscape Steps
- Zen Garden
- Backyard Fire Pit

Gallery

Large slabs of stone are stacked to create broad landscape steps that will last for generations. You'll want to hire a contractor to work with anything this heavy.

Neatly laid sandstone pavers or even a cast concrete walkway can add new lines and interesting textures to your garden.

A permeable paver driveway has gaps between paver units to help prevent water runoff from reaching the storm sewers.

Cast and natural stone can be combined effectively, but be sure to put plenty of thought into it before you commit. Mixing landscape elements can backfire as easily as it can succeed.

A "statement" boulder adds drama to this Zen-inspired garden space.

Loose-laid, freeform flagstones form a more casual, naturalistic walkway than cut stones. If you like doing jigsaw puzzles you'll enjoy this project.

This drystack, ashlar retaining wall is topped with capstones that create shelves for potted plants. Using the wall to terrace the hillside makes planning and maintenance much easier.

Selected carefully and placed thoughtfully, a few boulders and specimen stones have a very similar visual effect to specimen plants and shrubberies.

Brick pavers complement the brick siding on this house to create an inviting transition between the house and yard.

Drystack walls often are fitted with mortared caps to help hold the wall together and to make the top more useful as a resting spot.

Interlocking concrete block is the most common material used to make retaining walls these days. The blocks are easy to work with as long as you have a relatively strong back.

A stone wall rounds off and defines this intimate patio space.

Interlocking Block Retaining Wall

Think of retaining walls as shelves in your landscape where colorful plants can be on display, or as layers that carve nooks out of a sloped area to make the space more user-friendly. The fact is, keeping grass alive on a steep slope is virtually mission impossible. You can prevent erosion and form levels of usable space by building a retaining wall, or series of walls.

Retaining walls may be functional—serving to literally "retain" land at various levels on a slope; or purely aesthetic, as a way to add visual, vertical interest to a flat landscape. In this case, you'll be bringing in soil to backfill the retaining wall. Regardless of the reason for building a retaining wall, the materials available today make the job much like putting together a puzzle. You don't need mortar, and you can find interlocking block in various textures and colors that complement existing architectural features. Some types of block simply stack, while others are held together by an overlapping system of flanges. These flanges automatically set the backward pitch as blocks are stacked. Still, some blocks use fiberglass pins.

Tools & Materials ▸

Wheelbarrow	Masonry chisel	Tape measure	Perforated drain pipe
Shovel	Eye protection	Marking pencil	Coarse backfill
Garden rake	Hearing protectors	Caulk gun	material
Line level	Work gloves	Stakes	Construction adhesive
Hand tamper	Circular saw with	Mason's string	Retaining wall block
Tamping machine	masonry-cutting blade	Landscape fabric	Cap blocks
Small maul	Level	Compactable gravel	Spraypaint

Terraced retaining walls work well on steep hillsides. Two or more short retaining walls are easier to install and more stable than a single, tall retaining wall. Construct the terraces so each wall is no higher than 3 ft.

Design Considerations

If your slope exceeds four feet in height, create a terrace effect with a series of retaining walls. Build the first retaining wall, then progress up the slope and build the next, allowing several feet between layers. The bleacher effect provides shelves for plantings and reduces erosion.

If your retaining wall will exceed four feet in height, consider bringing in a professional to assist with the job. The higher the wall, the more pressure—thousands of pounds—it must withstand from soil and water. Also, significant walls may require a building permit or specially engineered design. Keep in mind,

interlocking block weights up to 80 pounds each, so you'll want to draft some helpers regardless of the project height. You can use cut stone rather than interlocking block and the project steps are the same. Both materials are durable and easy to work with.

Finally, tune into potential drainage issues before breaking ground. A wall can be damaged when water saturates the soil behind block or stone. You may need to dig a drainage swale in low-lying areas before beginning. This project includes a drain pipe to usher water away from the wall.

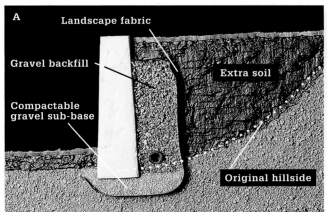
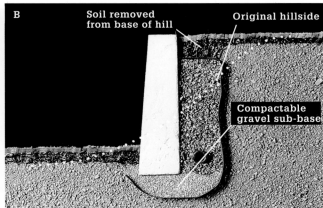

Increase the level area above the wall (A) by positioning the wall well forward from the top of the hill. Fill in behind the wall with extra soil, which is available from sand-and-gravel companies. Keep the basic shape of your yard (B) by positioning the wall near the top of the hillside. Use the soil removed at the base of the hill to fill in near the top of the wall.

Building Retaining Walls ▸

Backfill with crushed stone and install a perforated drain pipe about 6" above the bottom of the backfill. Vent the pipe to the side or bottom of the retaining wall, where runoff water can flow away from the hillside without causing erosion.

Make a stepped trench when the ends of a retaining wall must blend into an existing hillside. Retaining walls often are designed so the ends curve or turn back into the slope.

How to Build a Retaining Wall Using Interlocking Block

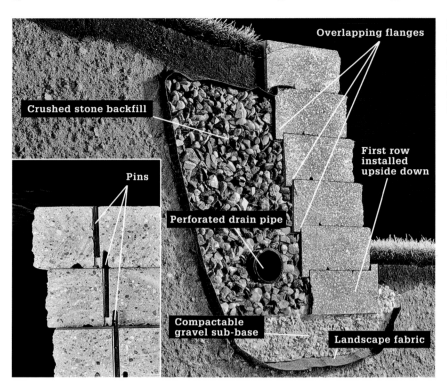

Crushed stone backfill

Overlapping flanges

First row installed upside down

Pins

Perforated drain pipe

Compactable gravel sub-base

Landscape fabric

Interlocking wall blocks do not need mortar. Some types are held together with a system of overlapping flanges that automatically set the backward pitch (batter) as the blocks are stacked, as shown in this project. Other types of blocks use fiberglass pins (inset).

1

Excavate the hillside, if necessary. Allow 12" of space for crushed stone backfill between the back of the wall and the hillside. Use stakes to mark the front edge of the wall. Connect the stakes with mason's string, and use a line level to check for level.

2

Dig out the bottom of the excavation below ground level, so it is 6" lower than the height of the block. For example, if you use 6"-thick block, dig down 12". Measure down from the string to make sure the bottom base is level.

3

Line the excavation with strips of landscape fabric cut 3 ft. longer than the planned height of the wall. Make sure all seams overlap by at least 6".

Spread a 6" layer of compactable gravel over the bottom of the excavation as a sub-base and pack it thoroughly. A rented tamping machine, or jumping jack, works better than a hand tamper for packing the sub-base.

Lay the first course of block, aligning the front edges with the mason's string. (When using flanged block, place the first course upside down and backward.) Check frequently with a level, and adjust, if necessary, by adding or removing sub-base material below the blocks.

Lay the second course of block according to manufacturer's instructions, checking to make sure the blocks are level. (Lay flanged block with the flanges tight against the underlying course.) Add 3 to 4" of gravel behind the block, and pack it with a hand tamper.

Make half-blocks for the corners and ends of a wall and use them to stagger vertical joints between courses. Score full blocks with a circular saw and masonry blade, and then break the blocks along the scored line with a maul and chisel.

(continued)

Add and tamp crushed stone, as needed, to create a slight downward pitch (about ¼" of height per foot of pipe) leading to the drain pipe outlet. Place the drain pipe on the crushed stone, 6" behind the wall, with the perforations face down. Make sure the pipe outlet is unobstructed. Lay courses of block until the wall is about 18" above ground level, staggering the vertical joints.

Fill behind the wall with crushed stone, and pack it thoroughly with the hand tamper. Lay the remaining courses of block, except for the cap row, backfilling with crushed stone and packing with the tamper as you go.

Before laying the cap block, fold the end of the landscape fabric over the crushed stone backfill. Add a thin layer of topsoil over the fabric, and then pack it thoroughly with a hand tamper. Fold any excess landscape fabric back over the tamped soil.

Apply landscape construction adhesive to the top course of block, and then lay the cap block. Use topsoil to fill in behind the wall and to fill in the base at the front of the wall. Install sod or plants as desired.

How to Add a Curve to an Interlocking Block Retaining Wall

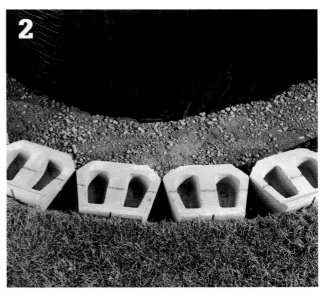

Outline the curve by first driving a stake at each end and then driving another stake at the point where lines extended from the first stakes would form a right angle. Tie a mason's string to the right-angle stake, extended to match the distance to the other two stakes, establishing the radius of the curve. Mark the curve by swinging flour or spray paint at the string end, like a compass.

Excavate for the wall section, following the curved layout line. To install the first course of landscape blocks, turn them upside down and backwards and align them with the radius curve. Use a 4-ft. level to ensure the blocks sit level and are properly placed.

Install subsequent courses so the overlapping flange sits flush against the back of the blocks in the course below. As you install each course, the radius will change because of the backwards pitch of the wall, affecting the layout of the courses. Where necessary, trim blocks to size. Install using landscape construction adhesive, taking care to maintain the running bond.

Use half blocks or cut blocks to create finished ends on open ends of the wall.

Stone Retaining Wall

Rough-cut wall stones may be dry stacked (without mortar) into retaining walls, garden walls, and other stonescape features. Dry-stack walls are able to move and shift with the frost, and they also drain well so they don't require deep footings and drainage tiles. Unlike fieldstone and boulder walls, short wall-stone walls can be just a single stone thick.

In the project featured here, we use rough-split limestone blocks about eight by four inches thick and in varying lengths. Walls like this may be built up to three feet tall, but keep them shorter if you can, to be safe. Building multiple short walls is often a more effective way to manage a slope than to build one taller wall. Called terracing, this practice requires some planning. Ideally, the flat ground between pairs of walls will be approximately the uniform size.

A dry-laid natural stone retaining wall is a very organic-looking structure compared to interlocking block retaining walls (see page 134). One way to exploit the natural look is to plant some of your favorite stone-garden perennials in the joints as you build the wall(s). Usually one plant or a cluster of three will add interest to a wall without suffocating it in vegetation or compromising its stability. Avoid plants that get very large or develop thick, woody roots or stems that may compromise the stability of the wall.

A well-built retaining wall has a slight lean, called a batter, back into the slope. It has a solid base and the bottom course is dug in behind the lower terrace.

Drainage gravel can help keep the soil from turning to mud, which will slump and press against the wall.

The same basic techniques used to stack natural stone in a retaining wall may be used for building a short garden wall as well. Obviously, there is no need for drainage allowances or wall returns in a garden wall. Simply prepare a base similar to the one shown here and begin stacking. The wall will look best if it wanders and meanders a bit. Unless you're building a very short wall (less than 18 inches), use two parallel courses that lean against one another for the basic construction. Cap it with flat capstones that run the full width of the wall (see page 144).

Tools & Materials ▸

Goggles	Garden rake
Gloves	Torpedo level
Steel-toe boots	Straight 2 × 4
Mattock with pick	Hand tamper
Hatchet or loppers	Compactable gravel
Spades	Ashlar wall stone
Measuring tape	Drainage gravel
Mason's string	Landscape fabric
Line level	Block-and-stone adhesive
Stakes	Caulk gun
Hand maul	

A natural stone retaining wall not only adds a stunning framework to your landscape, but it also lends a practical hand to prevent hillsides and slopes from deteriorating over time.

Cross Sections: Stone Retaining Walls

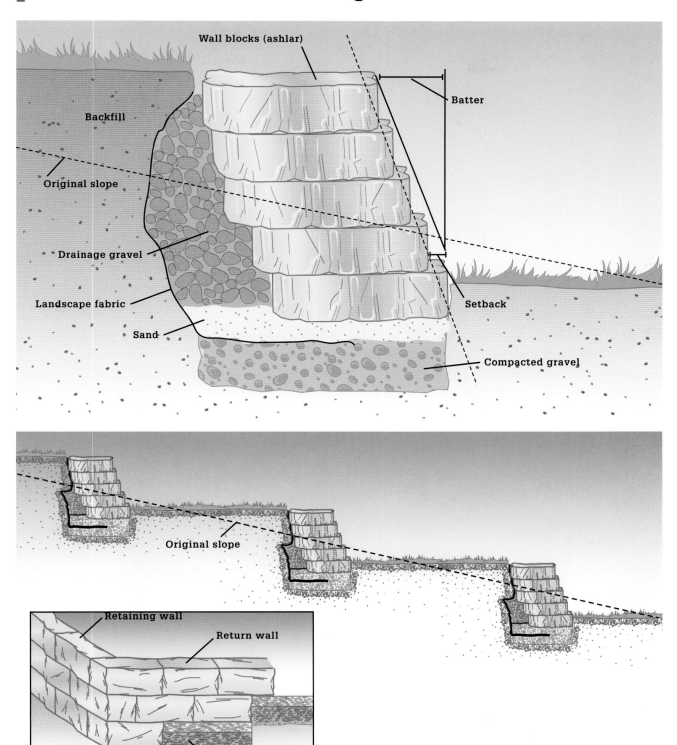

Wall blocks (ashlar)

Batter

Backfill

Original slope

Drainage gravel

Landscape fabric

Sand

Setback

Compacted gravel

Original slope

Retaining wall

Return wall

Compacted base

A stone retaining wall breaks up a slope to neat flat lawn areas that are more usable (top). A series of walls and terraces (bottom) break up larger slopes. Short return walls (inset) create transitions to the yard.

How to How to Build a Stone Retaining Wall

Dig into the slope to create a trench for the first wall. Reserve the soil you remove nearby—you'll want to backfill with it when the wall is done.

Level the bottom of the trench and measure to make sure you've excavated deeply enough.

After compacting a base, cover the trench and hill slope with landscape fabric, and then pour and level a 1" layer of coarse sand.

Place the first course of stones in rough position. Run a level mason's string at the average height of the stones.

Add or remove gravel under each stone to bring the front edges level with the mason's string.

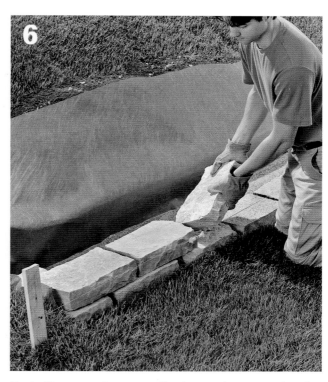

Begin the second course with a longer stone on each end so the vertical gaps between stones are staggered over the first course.

Finish out the second course. Use shards and chips of stone as shims where needed to stabilize the stones. Check to make sure the ½" setback is followed.

Finish setting the return stones in the second course, making adjustments as needed for the return to be level.

(continued)

Backfill behind the wall with river rock or another good drainage rock.

Fold the landscape fabric over the drainage rock (the main job of the fabric is to keep soil from migrating into the drainage rock and out the wall) and backfill behind it with soil to level the ground.

Trim the landscape fabric just behind the back of the wall, near the top.

Finish the wall by capping it off with some of your nicer, long flat stones. Bond them with block-and-stone adhesive.

13

Level off the soil behind the wall with a garden rake. Add additional walls if you are terracing.

Planting Your Retaining Wall ▸

Natural stone retaining walls look quite lovely in their own right. However, you can enhance the effect by making some well-chosen planting choices for the wall itself. You can plan for this in the wall construction by leaving an extra wide gap between two stones in one of the courses and then planting in the gap. Or you can replace a stone in the wall with a shorter one, also creating a gap. To plant a gap, cut the fabric and set a good-size, bare-root perennial of an appropriate species to the bottom of this joint. Fan out the roots over the soil and use sphagnum moss to plug up the gaps in the wall around plants. Adhere the stone in the next course that bridges the gap with block-and-stone adhesive. Keep plants well watered until established. Eventually, the plant roots will hold the soil instead of the moss.

Set plants in natural-looking clusters of the same species. Do not suffocate the wall with too many plants.

Drystack Stone Wall

Stone walls are beautiful, long-lasting structures that are surprisingly easy to build provided you plan carefully. A low stone wall can be constructed without mortar using a centuries-old method known as dry laying. With this technique, the wall is actually formed by two separate stacks that lean together slightly. The position and weight of the two stacks support each other, forming a single, sturdy wall. A dry stone wall can be built to any length, but its width must be at least half of its height.

You can purchase stone for this project from a quarry or stone supplier, where different sizes, shapes, and colors of stone are sold, priced by the ton. The quarry or stone center can also sell you Type M mortar—necessary for bonding the capstones to the top of the wall.

Building dry stone walls requires patience and a fair amount of physical effort. The stones must be sorted by size and shape. You'll probably also need to shape some of the stones to achieve consistent spacing and a general appearance that appeals to you.

To shape a stone, score it using a circular saw outfitted with a masonry blade. Place a mason's chisel on the score line and strike with a maul until the stone breaks. Wear safety glasses when using stonecutting tools.

Tools & Materials ▸

Mason's string and stakes
Compactable gravel
Ashlar stone
Capstones
Mortar mix

Trowel
Stiff-bristle brush
Work gloves
Protective footwear

It is easiest to build a dry stone wall with ashlar—stone that has been split into roughly rectangular blocks. Ashlar stone is stacked in the same running-bond pattern used in brick wall construction; each stone overlaps a joint in the previous course. This technique avoids long vertical joints, resulting in a wall that is attractive and also strong.

How to Build a Dry Stone Wall

Lay out the wall site using stakes and mason's string. Dig a 6"-deep trench that extends 6" beyond the wall on all sides. Add a 4" crushed stone sub-base to the trench, creating a "V" shape by sloping the sub-base so the center is about 2" deeper than the edges.

Select appropriate stones and lay the first course. Place pairs of stones side by side, flush with the edges of the trench and sloping toward the center. Use stones of similar height; position uneven sides face down. Fill any gaps between the shaping stones with small filler stones.

Lay the next course, staggering the joints. Use pairs of stones of varying lengths to offset the center joint. Alternate stone length, and keep the height even, stacking pairs of thin stones if necessary to maintain consistent height. Place filler stones in the gaps.

Tie stones

Every other course, place a tie stone every 3 ft. You may need to split the tie stones to length. Check the wall periodically for level.

Mortar the capstones to the top of the wall, keeping the mortar at least 6" from the edges so it's not visible. Push the capstones together and mortar the cracks in between. Brush off dried excess mortar with a stiff-bristle brush.

Mortared Stone Wall

The mortared stone wall is a classic that brings structure and appeal to any yard or garden. Square-hewn ashlar and bluestone are the easiest to build with, though fieldstone and rubble also work well and make attractive walls.

Because the mortar turns the wall into a monolithic structure that can crack and heave with a freeze-thaw cycle, a concrete footing is required for a mortared stone wall. To maintain strength in the wall, use the heaviest, thickest stones for the base of the wall and thinner, flatter stones for the cap.

As you plan the wall layout, install tie stones—stones that span the width of the wall (page 147)—about every three feet, staggered through the courses both vertically and horizontally throughout the wall. Use the squarest, flattest stones to build the "leads," or ends of the wall first, and then fill the middle courses. Plan for joints around one inch thick and make sure joints in successive courses do not line up. Follow this rule of thumb: Cover joints below with a full stone above; locate joints above over a full stone below.

Laying a mortared stone wall is labor-intensive but satisfying work. Make sure to work safely and enlist friends to help with the heavy lifting.

Tools & Materials ›

Tape measure
Pencil
Chalk line
Small whisk broom
Tools for mixing mortar
Maul
Stone chisel
Pitching chisel
Trowel
Jointing tool
Line level
Sponge
Garden hose

Concrete materials
　for foundation
Ashlar stone
Type N or
　Type S mortar
Stakes and
　mason's line
Scrap wood
Muriatic acid
Bucket of water
Sponge
Eye protection
　and work gloves

A mortared stone wall made from ashlar adds structure and classic appeal to your home landscape. Plan carefully and enlist help to ease the building process.

How to Build a Mortared Stone Wall

Pour a footing for the wall and allow it to cure for one week. Measure and mark the wall location so it is centered on the footing. Snap chalk lines along the length of the footing for both the front and the back faces of the wall. Lay out corners using the 3-4-5 right angle method.

Dry-lay the entire first course. Starting with a tie stone at each end, arrange stones in two rows along the chalk lines with joints about 1" thick. Use smaller stones to fill the center of the wall. Use larger, heavier stones in the base and lower courses. Place additional tie stones approximately every 3 ft. Trim stones as needed.

Mix a stiff batch of Type N or Type S mortar, following the manufacturer's directions (pages 18 to 19). Starting at an end or corner, set aside some of the stone and brush off the foundation. Spread an even, 2" thick layer of mortar onto the foundation, about ½" from the chalk lines—the mortar will squeeze out a little.

Firmly press the first tie stone into the mortar so it is aligned with the chalk lines and relatively level. Tap the top of the stone with the handle of the trowel to set it. Continue to lay stones along each chalk line, working to the opposite end of the wall.

(continued)

After installing the entire first course, fill voids along the center of the wall that are larger than 2" with smaller rubble. Fill the remaining spaces and joints with mortar, using the trowel.

As you work, rake the joints using a scrap of wood to a depth of ½"; raking joints highlights the stones rather than the mortared joints. After raking, use a whisk broom to even the mortar in the joints.

Variation: You can also tool joints for a cleaner, tighter mortared joint. Tool joints when your thumb can leave an imprint in the mortar without removing any of it.

Drive stakes at the each end of the wall and align a mason's line with the face of the wall. Use a line level to level the string at the height of the next course. Build up each end of the wall, called the "leads," making sure to stagger the joints between courses. Check the leads with a 4-ft. level on each wall face to make sure it is plumb.

If heavy stones push out too much mortar, use wood wedges cut from scrap to hold the stone in place. Once the mortar sets up, remove the wedges and fill the voids with fresh mortar.

Removing Mortar ▶

Have a bucket of water and a sponge handy in case mortar oozes or spills onto the face of the stone. Wipe mortar away immediately before it can harden.

9

Fill the middle courses between the leads by first dry laying stones for placement and then mortaring them in place. Install tie stones about every 3 ft., both vertically and horizontally, staggering their position in each course. Make sure joints in successive courses do not fall in alignment.

10

Install cap stones by pressing flat stones that span the width of the wall into a mortar bed. Do not rake the joints, but clean off excess mortar with the trowel and clean excess mortar from the surface of the stones using a damp sponge.

11

Allow the wall to cure for one week, and then clean it using a solution of 1 part muriatic acid and 10 parts water. Wet the wall using a garden hose, apply the acid solution, and then immediately rinse with plenty of clean, clear water. Always wear goggles, long sleeves and pants, and heavy rubber gloves when using acids.

Repairing a Stone Wall

Damage to stonework is typically caused by frost heave, erosion or deterioration of mortar, or by stones that have worked out of place. Dry-stone walls are more susceptible to erosion and popping while mortared walls develop cracks that admit water, which can freeze and cause further damage.

Inspect stone structures once a year for signs of damage and deterioration. Replacing a stone or repointing crumbling mortar now will save you work in the long run.

A leaning stone column or wall probably suffers from erosion or foundation problems and can be dangerous if neglected. If you have the time, you can tear down and rebuild dry-laid structures, but mortared structures with excessive lean need professional help.

Stones in a wall can become dislodged due to soil settling, erosion, or seasonal freeze-thaw cycles. Make the necessary repairs before the problem migrates to other areas.

Tools & Materials ▸

Maul
Chisel
Camera
Shovel
Hand tamper
Level
Batter gauge
Stiff-bristle brush
Trowels for mixing
   and pointing
Mortar bag

Masonry chisels
Wood shims
Carpet-covered
   2 × 4
Chalk
Compactable gravel
Replacement stones
Type M mortar
Mortar tint
Eye protection
Work gloves

Repairing Popped Stones ▸

Return a popped stone to its original position. If other stones have settled in its place, drive shims between neighboring stones to make room for the popped stone. Be careful not to wedge too far.

Use a 2 × 4 covered with carpet to avoid damaging the stone when hammering it into place. After hammering, make sure a replacement stone hasn't damaged or dislodged the adjoining stones.

How to Rebuild a Dry-stone Wall Section

Study the wall and determine how much of it needs to be rebuilt. Plan to dismantle the wall in a V shape, centered on the damaged section. Number each stone and mark its orientation with chalk so you can rebuild it following the original design. *Tip: Photograph the wall, making sure the markings are visible.*

Capstones are often set in a mortar bed atop the last course of stone. You may need to chip out the mortar with a maul and chisel to remove the capstones. Remove the marked stones, taking care to check the overall stability of the wall as you work.

Erosion ▶

Rebuild the wall, one course at a time, using replacement stones only when necessary. Start each course at the ends and work toward the center. On thick walls, set the face stones first, and then fill in the center with smaller stones. Check your work with a level and use a batter gauge to maintain the batter of the wall. If your capstones were mortared, re-lay them in fresh mortar. Wash off the chalk with water and a stiff-bristle brush.

If you're rebuilding because of erosion, dig a trench at least 6" deep under the damaged area, and fill it with compactable gravel. Tamp the gravel with a hand tamper. This will improve drainage and prevent water from washing soil out from beneath the wall.

Tips for Repairing Mortared Stone Walls

Tint mortar for repair work so it blends with the existing mortar. Mix several samples of mortar, adding a different amount of tint to each and allow them to dry thoroughly. Compare each sample to the old mortar and choose the closest match.

Use a mortar bag to restore weathered and damaged mortar joints over an entire structure. Remove loose mortar (see below) and clean all surfaces with a stiff-bristle brush and water. Dampen the joints before tuck-pointing and cover all of the joints, smoothing and brushing as necessary.

How to Repoint Mortar Joints

Carefully rake out cracked and crumbling mortar, stopping when you reach solid mortar. Remove loose mortar and debris with a stiff-bristle brush. *Tip: Rake the joints with a chisel and maul or make your own raking tool by placing an old screwdriver in a vise and bending the shaft about 45°.*

Mix Type M mortar, and then dampen the repair surfaces with clean water. Working from the top down, pack mortar into the crevices using a pointing trowel. Smooth the mortar when it has set up enough to resist light finger pressure. Remove excess mortar with a stiff-bristle brush.

How to Replace a Mortared Stone Wall

Remove the damaged stone by chiseling out the surrounding mortar using a masonry chisel or a modified screwdriver (opposite page). Drive the chisel toward the damaged stone to avoid harming neighboring stones. Once the stone is out, chisel the surfaces inside the cavity as smooth as possible.

Brush out the cavity to remove loose mortar and debris. Test the surrounding mortar and chisel or scrape out any mortar that isn't firmly bonded.

Dry-fit the replacement stone. The stone should be stable in the cavity and blend with the rest of the wall. You can mark the stone with chalk and cut it to fit, but excessive cutting will result in a conspicuous repair.

Mist the stone and cavity lightly, and then apply Type M mortar around the inside of the cavity using a trowel. Butter all mating sides of the replacement stone. Insert the stone and wiggle it forcefully to remove any air pockets. Use a pointing trowel to pack the mortar solidly around the stone. Smooth the mortar when it has set up.

Loose Rock Landscape Path

Loose-fill gravel pathways are perfect for stone gardens, casual yards, and other situations where a hard surface is not required. The material is inexpensive, and its fluidity accommodates curves and irregular edging. Since gravel may be made from any rock, gravel paths may be matched to larger stones in the environment, tying them in to your landscaping. The gravel you choose need not be restricted to stone, either. Industrial and agricultural byproducts, such as cinder and ashes, walnut shells, seashells, and ceramic fragments may also be used as path material.

For a more stable path, choose angular or jagged gravel over rounded materials. However, if your preference is to stroll throughout your landscape barefoot, your feet will be better served with smoother stones, such as river rock or pond pebbles. With stone, look for a crushed product in the ¼ to ¾" range. Angular or smooth, stones smaller than that can be tracked into the house, while larger materials are uncomfortable and potentially hazardous to walk on. If it complements your landscaping, use light-colored gravel, such as buff limestone. Visually, it is much easier to follow a light pathway at night because it reflects more moonlight.

Stable edging helps keep the pathway gravel from migrating into the surrounding mulch and soil. When integrated with landscape fabric, the edge keeps invasive perennials and trees from sending roots and shoots into the path. Do not use gravel paths near plants and trees that produce messy fruits, seeds, or other debris that will be difficult to remove from the gravel. Organic matter left on gravel paths will eventually rot into compost that will support weed growth.

A base of compactable gravel under the surface material keeps the pathway firm underfoot. For best results, embed the surface gravel material into the paver base with a plate compactor. This prevents the base from showing through if the gravel at the surface is disturbed. An underlayment of landscape fabric helps stabilize the pathway and blocks weeds, but if you don't mind pulling an occasional dandelion and are building on firm soil, it can be omitted.

Tools & Materials ▸

Mason's string	Edging
Hose or rope	Spikes
Marking paint	Professional-grade
Excavation tools	landscape fabric
Garden rake	Compactable gravel
Plate compactor	Dressed gravel
Sod stripper or	Eye and ear
power sod cutter	protection
Wood stakes	Work gloves
Lumber (1 × 2,	Circular saw
2 × 4)	Maul
Straight 2 × 4	

Construction Details

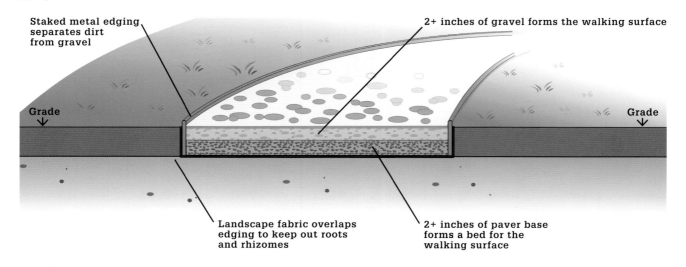

Staked metal edging separates dirt from gravel

2+ inches of gravel forms the walking surface

Grade

Grade

Landscape fabric overlaps edging to keep out roots and rhizomes

2+ inches of paver base forms a bed for the walking surface

Loose materials can be used as filler between solid surface materials, like flagstone, or laid as the primary ground cover, as shown here.

Make a Spacer Gauge ▸

To ensure that the edges of the pathway are exactly parallel, create a spacer bar and use it as a guide to install the edging. Start with a piece of 2 × 4 that's a bit longer than the path width. Near one end, cut a notch that will fit snugly over the edging. Trim the spacer so the distance from the notch to the other end is the planned width of the pathway.

How to Create a Gravel Pathway

Lay out one edge of the path excavation. Use a section of hose or rope to create curves, and use stakes and string to indicate straight sections. Cut 1 × 2 spacers to set the path width and establish the second pathway edge; use another hose and/or more stakes and string to lay out the other edge. Mark both edges with marking paint.

Remove sod in the walkway area using a sod stripper or a power sod cutter (see option, at right). Excavate the soil to a depth of 4 to 6". Measure down from a 2 × 4 placed across the path bed to fine-tune the excavation. Grade the bottom of the excavation flat using a garden rake. *Note: If mulch will be used outside the path, make the excavation shallower by the depth of the mulch.* Compact the soil with a plate compactor.

Option: Use a power sod cutter to strip grass from your pathway site. Available at most rental centers and large home centers, sod cutters excavate to a very even depth. The cut sod can be replanted in other parts of your lawn.

Lay landscaping fabric from edge to edge, lapping over the undisturbed ground on either side of the path. On straight sections, you may be able to run parallel to the path with a single strip; on curved paths, it's easier to lay the fabric perpendicular to the path. Overlap all seams by 6".

Install edging over the fabric. Shim the edging with small stones, if necessary, so the top edge is ½" above grade (if the path passes through grass) or 2" above grade (if it passes through a mulched area). Secure the edging with spikes. To install the second edge, use a 2 × 4 spacer gauge that's been notched to fit over your edging (see facing page).

Stone or vertical-brick edges may be set in deeper trenches at the sides of the path. Place these on top of the fabric also. You do not have to use additional edging with paver edging, but metal (or other) edging will keep the pavers from wandering.

(continued)

Trim excess fabric, then backfill behind the edging with dirt and tamp it down carefully with the end of a 2 × 4. This secures the edging and helps it to maintain its shape.

Add a 2- to 4"-thick layer of compactable gravel over the entire pathway. Rake the gravel flat. Then, spread a thin layer of your surface material over the base gravel.

Tamp the base and surface gravel together using a plate compactor. Be careful not to disturb or damage the edging with the compactor.

Fill in the pathway with the remaining surface gravel. Drag a 2 × 4 across the tops of the edging using a sawing motion, to level the gravel flush with the edging.

Set the edging brick flush with the gravel using a mallet and 2 × 4.

Tamp the surface again using the plate compactor or a hand tamper. Compact the gravel so it is slightly below the top of the edging. This will help keep the gravel from migrating out of the path.

Rinse off the pathway with a hose to wash off dirt and dust and bring out the true colors of the materials.

Stepping Stone Landscape Path

A stepping stone path is both a practical and appealing way to traverse a landscape. With large stones as foot landings, you are free to use pretty much any type of fill material in between. You could even place stepping stones on individual footings over ponds and streams, making water the temporary infill that surrounds the stones. The infill does not need to follow a narrow path bed, either. Steppers can be used to cross a broad expanse of gravel, such as a Zen gravel panel or a smaller graveled opening in an alpine rock garden.

Stepping stones in a path serve two purposes: they lead the eye, and they carry the traveler. In both cases, the goal is rarely fast, direct transport, but more of a relaxing stroll that's comfortable, slow-paced, and above all, natural. Arrange the stepping stones in your walking path according to the gaits and strides of the people that are most likely to use the pathway. Keep in mind that our gaits tend to be longer on a utility path than in a rock garden.

Sometimes steppers are placed more for visual effect, with the knowledge that they will break the pacing rule with artful clusters of stones. Clustering is also an effective way to slow or congregate walkers near a fork in the path or at a good vantage point for a striking feature of the garden.

In the project featured here, landscape edging is used to contain the loose infill material (small aggregate), however a stepping stone path can also be effective without edging. For example, setting a series of steppers directly into your lawn and letting the lawn grass grow between them is a great choice as well.

Tools & Materials ▶

Mason's string	Thick steppers or
Hose or rope	broad river rocks
Marking paint	with one flat face
Sod stripper	¼ to ½" pond
Excavation tools	pebbles
Hand tamp	2½"-dia. river rock
Wood stakes	Eye and ear
1 × 2 lumber	protection
Straight 2 × 4	Work gloves
Edging	Level
Landscape fabric	Rake
Coarse sand	

Choosing Steppers ▶

Select beefy stones (minimum 2½ to 3½" thick) with at least one flat side. Thinner stepping stones tend to sink into the pebble infill. Stones that are described as stepping stones usually have two flat faces. For the desired visual effect on this project, we chose steppers and 12 to 24" wide fieldstones with one broad, flat face (the rounded face is buried in the ground, naturally).

Fieldstone with a flat face

Steppers

Stepping stones blend beautifully into many types of landscaping, including rock gardens, ponds, flower or vegetable gardens, or manicured grass lawns.

How to Make a Pebbled Stepping Stone Path

Excavate and prepare a bed for the path as you would for the gravel pathway (see pages 158 to 159), but use coarse building sand instead of compactable gravel for the base layer. Screed the sand flat so it's 2" below the top of the edging. Do not tamp the sand. *Tip: Low-profile plastic landscape edging is a good choice because it does not compete with the pathway.*

Moisten the sand bed, then position the stepping stones in the sand, spacing them for comfortable walking and the desired appearance. As you work, place a 2 × 4 across three adjacent stones to make sure they are even with one another. Add or remove sand beneath the steppers, as needed, to stabilize and level the stones.

Pour in a layer of larger infill stones (2"-dia. river rock is seen here). Smooth the stones with a garden rake. The infill should be below the tops of the stepping stones. Reserve about ⅓ of the larger diameter rocks.

Add the smaller infill stones, that will migrate down and fill in around the larger infill rocks. To help settle the rocks, you can tamp lightly with a hand tamper, but don't get too aggressive—the larger rocks might fracture easily.

Scatter the remaining large infill stones across the infill area so they float on top of the other stones. Eventually, they will sink down lower in the pathway and you will need to lift and replace them selectively to maintain the original appearance.

Variations

Move from a formal space to a less orderly area of your landscape by creating a pathway that begins with closely spaced steppers on the formal end and gradually transforms into a mostly-gravel path on the casual end, with only occasional clusters of steppers.

Combine concrete stepping pavers with crushed rock or other small stones for a path with a cleaner, more contemporary look. Follow the same basic techniques used on these two pages, setting the pavers first, then filling in-between with the desired infill material(s).

Timber & Gravel Landscape Steps

Timberframed steps provide a delightfully simple and structurally satisfying way to manage slopes. They are usually designed with shallow steps that have long runs and large tread areas, that can be filled with a variety of materials. One popular method is gravel, shown here. Other tread surfaces you might consider are bricks, cobbles, stepping stones, or poured concrete. Even large flagstones can be cut to fit the tread openings.

Timber steps needn't follow the straight and narrow, either. You can vary the lengths of the left and right returns to create swooping helical steps that suggest spiral staircases. Or, increase the length of both returns to create a broad landing on which to set pots or accommodate a natural flattening of the slope. Want to soften the steps? Use soil as a base near the sides of the steps and plant herbs or ground cover. Or for a spring surprise, plant daffodils under a light pea gravel top dressing at the edges of the steps.

Timber steps don't require a frost footing, because the wooden joints flex with the earth rather than crack like solid concrete steps would. However, it's a good idea to include some underground anchoring to keep loose muddy soil from pushing the steps forward. To provide longterm stability, the gravel-filled steps shown here are secured to a timber cleat at the base of the slope, while concrete-filled steps are anchored at the base with long sections of pipe driven into the ground.

Designing steps is an important part of the process. Determine the total rise and run of the hill and translate this into a step size that conforms to this formula: $2\times$ (rise) + run = 26". Your step rise will equal your timber width, that can range from approximately $3\frac{1}{2}$" (for 4×4 timbers or 4×6 on the flat) to $7\frac{1}{4}$" or $7\frac{1}{2}$" (for 8×8 timbers). As with any steps, be sure to keep the step size consistent so people don't trip.

Tools & Materials ▶

Marking paint	Drill and ⅜" bit
Mason's string	with long shaft
Level	Wood stakes
Excavation tools	Compactable gravel
Hand tamp	2 × 4 lumber
Circular saw	Landscape timbers
Speed square	⅜" landscape spikes
Framing square	Gravel
Sledgehammer	

Here we use gravel (small aggregate river rock), a common surface for paths and rock gardens, for the tread surfaces. Other tread surfaces include bricks, cobbles, and stepping stones. Even large flagstones can be fit to the tread openings.

Construction Details

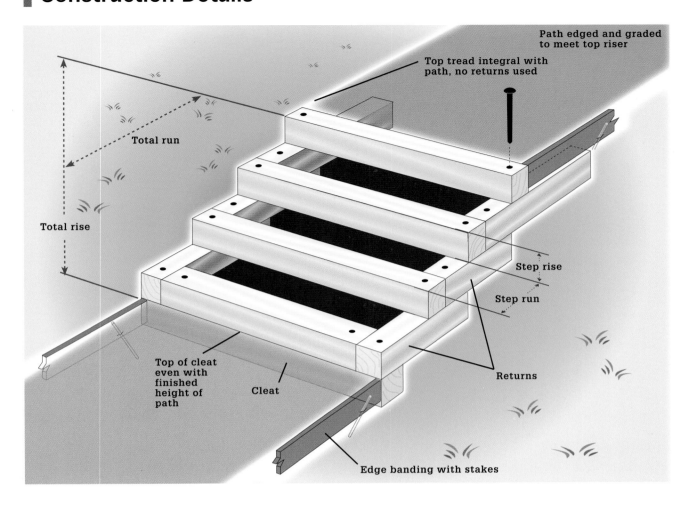

Path edged and graded to meet top riser

Top tread integral with path, no returns used

Total run

Total rise

Step rise

Step run

Top of cleat even with finished height of path

Cleat

Returns

Edge banding with stakes

How to Build Timber & Gravel Landscape Steps

Install and level the timber cleat: mark the outline of the steps onto the ground using marking paint. Dig a trench for the cleat at the base of the steps. Add 2 to 4" of compactable gravel in the trench and compact it with a hand tamp. Cut the cleat to length and set it into the trench. Add or remove gravel beneath the cleat so it is level and its top is even with the surrounding ground or path surface.

Create trenches filled with tamped gravel for the returns (the timbers running back into the hill, perpendicular to the cleat and risers). The returns should be long enough to anchor the riser and returns of the step above. Dig trenches back into the hill for the returns and compact 2 to 4" of gravel into the trenches so each return will sit level on the cleat and gravel.

(continued)

Cutting Timbers ▸

Large landscape timbers (6 × 6" and bigger) can be cut accurately and squarely with a circular saw, even though the saw's cutting capacity isn't big enough to do the job completely. First, draw cutting lines on all four sides of the timber using a speed square as guide. Next, cut along the line on all four sides with the saw set for maximum blade depth. Finally, use a hand saw to finish the cut. For most DIYers, this will yield a straighter cut than saws that can make the cut in one pass, such as a reciprocating saw.

Cut and position the returns and the first riser. Using a 2 × 4 as a level extender, check to see if the backs of the returns are level with each other and adjust by adding or removing gravel in the trenches. Drill four ⅜"-dia. holes and fasten the first riser and the two returns to the cleat with spikes.

Excavate and add tamped gravel for the second set of returns. Cut and position the second riser across the ends of the first returns, leaving the correct unit run between the riser faces. Note that only the first riser doesn't span the full width of the steps. Cut and position the returns, check for level, then pre-drill and spike the second riser and returns to the returns below.

Build the remaining steps in the same fashion. As you work, it may be necessary to alter the slope with additional excavating or backfilling (few natural hills follow a uniform slope). Add or remove soil as needed along the sides of the steps so that the returns are exposed roughly equally on both sides. Also, each tread should always be higher than the neighboring ground.

Install the final riser. Typically, the last timber does not have returns because its tread surface is integral with the path or surrounding ground. The top of this timber should be slightly higher than the ground. As an alternative, you can use returns to contain pathway material at the top of the steps.

Lay and tamp a base of compactable gravel in each step tread area. Use a 2 × 4 as a tamper. For proper compaction, tamp the gravel in 2" or thinner layers before adding more. Leave about 2" of space in each tread for the surface material.

Fill up the tread areas with gravel or other appropriate material. Irregular crushed gravel offers maximum surface stability, while smooth stones, like the river rock seen here, blend into the environment more naturally and feel better underfoot than crushed gravel and stone.

Create or improve pathways at the top and bottom of the steps. For a nice effect, build a loose-fill walkway using the same type of gravel that you used for the steps. Install a railing, if desired or if required by the local building code.

Flagstone Landscape Steps

Flagstone steps are perfect structures for managing natural slopes. Our design consists of broad flagstone treads and blocky ashlar risers, commonly sold as wall stone. The risers are prepared with compactable gravel beds on which the flagstone treads rest. For the project featured here, we purchased both the flagstone and the wall stone in their natural split state (as opposed to sawn). It may seem like overkill, but you should plan on purchasing 40 percent more flagstone, by square foot coverage, than your plans say you need. The process of fitting the stones together involves a lot of cutting and waste.

The average height of your risers is defined by the height of the wall stone available to you. These rough stones are separated and sold in a range of thicknesses (such as 3 to 4"), but hand-picking the stones helps bring them into a tighter range. The more uniform the thicknesses of your blocks, the less shimming and adjusting you'll have to do. (Remember, all of the steps must be the same size, to prevent a tripping hazard.) You will also need to stock up on slivers of rocks to use as shims to bring your risers and returns to a consistent height; breaking and cutting your stone generally produces plenty of these.

Flagstone steps work best when you create the broadest possible treads: think of them as a series of

terraced patios. The goal, once you have the stock in hand, is to create a tread surface with as few stones as possible. This generally means you'll be doing quite a bit of cutting to get the irregular shapes to fit together. For a more formal look, cut the flagstones along straight lines so they fit together with small, regular gaps.

Tools & Materials ▸

Tape measure	Compactable gravel
Mason's string	Wall stone
Marking paint	Flagstone
Line level	Stone chisels
Torpedo level	Stone and block
4-ft. level	adhesive
Excavation tools	Rubber mallet
Maul	Eye and ear
Hand tamp	protection
Wood stakes	Work gloves
Lumber (2 × 4,	Small brush
4× 4)	Spade
Straight 2 × 4	Coarse sand
Landscape fabric	

Construction Details

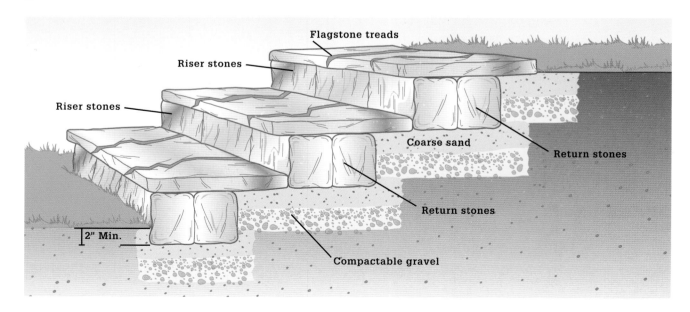

Flagstone treads

Riser stones

Riser stones

Coarse sand

Return stones

Return stones

2" Min.

Compactable gravel

How to Build Flagstone Garden Steps

Measure the height and length of the slope to calculate the rise and run dimensions for each step (see page 166 for help with designing and laying out steps). Plot the footprint of your steps on the ground using marking paint. Purchase wall stones for your risers and returns in a height equal to the rise of your steps. Also buy flagstone (with approx. 40% overage) for the step treads.

Begin the excavation for the area under the first riser and return stones by digging a trench to accommodate a 4" layer of gravel, plus the thickness of an average flagstone tread. For the area under the back edge of the first step's tread and the riser and return stones of the second step, dig to accommodate a 4" layer of gravel, plus a 1" layer of sand. Compact the soil with a 2 × 4 or 4 × 4.

Add a layer of compactable gravel to within 1" of the planned height and tamp. Add a top layer of compactable gravel and level it side to side and back to front. This top layer should be a flagstone's thickness below grade. This will keep the rise of the first step the same as the following steps. Leave the second layer of gravel uncompacted for easy adjustment of the riser and return stones.

Set the riser stones and one or two return stones onto the gravel base. Level the riser stones side to side by adding or removing gravel as needed. Level the risers front to back with a torpedo level. Allow for a slight up-slope for the returns (the steps should slope slightly downward from back to front so the treads will drain). Seat the stones firmly in the gravel with a hand maul, protecting the stone with a wood block.

(continued)

Line the excavated area for the first tread with landscape fabric, draping it to cover the insides of the risers and returns. Add layers of compactable gravel and tamp down to within 1" of the tops of the risers and returns. Fill the remainder of the bed with sand and level it side to side with a 2 × 4. Slope it slightly from back to front. This layer of sand should be a little above the first risers and returns so that the tread stones will compact down to sit on the wall stones.

Set the second group of risers and returns. First, measure the step/run distance back from the face of your first risers and set up a level mason's string across the sand bed. Position the second-step risers and returns as you did for the first step, except these don't need to be dug in on the bottom because the bottom tread will reduce the risers' effective height.

Fold the fabric over the tops of the risers and trim off the excess. Set the flagstone treads of the first step like a puzzle, leaving a consistent distance between stones. Use large, heavy stones with relatively straight edges at the front of the step, overhanging the risers by about 2".

Fill in with smaller stones near the back. Cut and dress stones where necessary using stone chisels and a maul or mason's hammer. Finding a good arrangement takes some trial and error. Strive for fairly regular gaps, and avoid using small stones as they are easily displaced. Ideally, all stones should be at least as large as a dinner plate.

Adjust the stones so the treads form a flat surface. Use a level as a guide, and add wet sand under thinner stones or remove sand from beneath thicker stones until all the flags come close to touching the level and are stable.

Shim between treads and risers with thin shards of stone. (Do not use sand to shim here). Glue the shards in place with block and stone adhesive. Check each step to make sure there is no path for sand to wash out from beneath the treads. You can settle smaller stones in sand with a mallet, but cushion your blows with a piece of wood.

Complete the second step in the same manner as the first. The bottoms of the risers should be at the same height as the bottoms of the tread on the step below. Continue building steps to the top of the slope. *Note: The top step often will not require returns.*

Fill the joints between stones with sand by sweeping the sand across the treads. Use coarse, dark sand such as granite sand, or choose polymeric sand, which resists washout better than regular builder's sand. Inspect the steps regularly for the first few weeks and make adjustments to the heights of stones as needed.

Zen Garden

What's commonly called a Zen garden in the West is actually a Japanese dry garden, with little historical connection to Zen Buddhism. The form typically consists of sparse, carefully positioned stones in a meticulously raked bed of coarse sand or fine gravel. Japanese dry gardens can be immensely satisfying. Proponents find the uncluttered space calming and the act of raking out waterlike ripples in the gravel soothing and perhaps even healing. The fact that they are low maintenance and drought resistant is another advantage.

Site your garden on flat or barely sloped ground away from messy trees and shrubs (and cats), as gravel and sand are eventually spoiled by the accumulation of organic matter. There are many materials you can use as the rakable medium for the garden. Generally, lighter-colored, very coarse sand is preferred—it needs to be small enough to be raked into rills yet large enough that the rake lines don't settle out immediately. Crushed

Tools & Materials ▸

Stakes
Mason's string
Garden hose
Landscape
    marking paint
Straight 2 × 4
Level
Measuring tape
Compactable gravel
Excavating tools

Crushed granite
    (light colored)
Hand maul
Manual tamper
Landscape fabric
Fieldstone steppers
Specimen stones
Border stones
Eye protection
    and work gloves

granite is a viable medium. Another option that is used occasionally is turkey grit, a fine gravel available from farm supply outlets. In this project, we show you how to edge your garden with cast pavers set on edge, although you may prefer to use natural stone blocks or even smooth stones in a range of four to six inches.

A Zen garden is a small rock garden, typically featuring a few large specimen stones inset into a bed of gravel. It gets its name from the meditative benefits of raking the gravel.

How to Make a Zen Garden

Lay out the garden location using stakes and string or hoses and then mark the outline directly onto the ground with landscape paint.

Excavate the site and install any large specimen stones that require burial more than ½ ft. below grade.

Dig a trench around the border for the border stones, and lay down landscape fabric.

Pour a 3" thick layer of compactable gravel into the border trench and tamp down with a post or a hand tamper.

(continued)

Place border blocks into the trench and adjust them so the tops are even.

Test different configurations of rocks in the garden to find an arrangement you like. If it's a larger garden, strategically place a few flat rocks so you can reach the entire garden with a rake without stepping in the raking medium.

Set the stones in position on individual beds of sand about 1" thick. Pour in pebbles.

Rake the medium into pleasing patterns with a special rake (see next page).

How to Make a Zen Garden Rake ▸

Once you have constructed your Zen garden, you will use two tools to interact with it: your eyes and a good rake. While any garden rake will suffice for creating the swirling and concentric rills that are hallmarks of the Zen garden, a special rake that's dedicated to the garden will enhance your hands-on interaction.

Many Zen garden rakes are constructed from bamboo. Bamboo is lightweight and readily available, especially through Internet sites. While you can certainly choose this material, you're likely to find that the lightness can actually work against it, causing you to exert more strain to cut through the raking medium. A rake made from solid wood has greater heft that lets it glide more smoothly through the medium. The rake shown here is made using only the following materials:

- 1¼"-dia. by 48" oak or pine dowel (handle)
- ½" by 36" oak or pine dowel (tines)
- 2 × 3 × 9½" piece of red oak (head)

Figure 1

Figure 2

Figure 3

Start by sanding all of the stock smooth using sandpaper up to 150 grit in coarseness. Soften the edges of the 2 × 3 with the sandpaper. Drill a 1¼" dia. hole in the head for the handle (Figure 1). The hole should go all the way through the head at a 22½° downward angle (half of a 45° angle), with the top of the hole no closer than ¾" to the top of the head. Use a backer board when drilling to prevent blowout and splinters.

Next, drill ½"-dia. by 1"-deep seat holes for the tines in the bottom edge of the blank. Locate centers of the two end holes 1" from the ends. Measure in 2½" from each end hole and mark centers for the intermediate tines. Use masking tape to mark a drilling depth of 1" on your drill bit and then drill perpendicular holes at each centerline.

Cut four 5"-long pieces of the ½"-dia. oak doweling for the tines. Apply wood glue into the bottom of each hole and insert the tines, setting them by gently tapping with a wood mallet (Figure 2). Then, apply glue to the handle hole's sides and insert the handle so the end protrudes all the way through. After the glue dries, drill a ½"-dia. hole down through the top of the head and into the handle. Glue a ½" dowel into the hole to reinforce the handle (this is called pinning).

Finally, use a back saw, gentleman's saw, or Japanese flush-cutting saw to trim the handle end and the handle pin flush with the head (Figure 3). Sand to smooth the trimmed ends and remove any dried glue. Finish with two or three light coats of wipe-on polyurethane tinted for red oak.

Backyard Fire Pit

A firepit is a backyard focal point and gathering spot. The one featured here is constructed around a metal liner, which will keep the fire pit walls from overheating and cracking if cooled suddenly by rain or a bucket of water. The liner here is a section of 36-inch-diameter corrugated culvert pipe. Check local codes for stipulations on pit area size. Many codes require a 20-foot-diameter pit area.

Ashlar wall stones add character to the fire pit walls, but you can use any type of stone, including cast concrete retaining wall blocks. You'll want to prep the base for the seating area as you dig the fire pit to be sure both rest on the same level plane.

Tools & Materials ▸

Wheelbarrow
Landscape paint
String and stakes
Spades
Metal pipe
Landscape edging
Level
Garden rake
Plate vibrator

Metal firepit liner
Compactable gravel
Top-dressing rock
 (trap rock)
Wall stones
Eye protection
 and work gloves

Some pointers to consider when using your fire pit include: 1) Make sure there are no bans or restrictions in effect; 2) Evaluate wind conditions and avoid building a fire if winds are heavy and/or blowing toward your home; 3) Keep shovels, sand, water, and a fire extinguisher nearby; 4) Extinguish fire with water and never leave the fire pit unattended.

Cross Section: Firepit

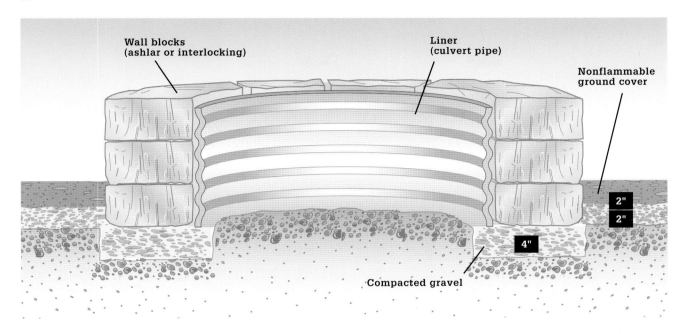

Wall blocks
(ashlar or interlocking)

Liner
(culvert pipe)

Nonflammable
ground cover

2"

2"

4"

Compacted gravel

Plan View: Firepit

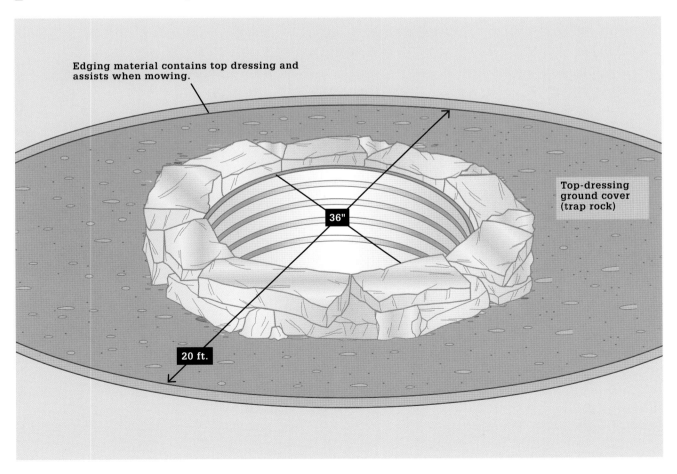

Edging material contains top dressing and
assists when mowing.

Top-dressing
ground cover
(trap rock)

36"

20 ft.

How to Build a Firepit

Outline the location for your firepit and the firepit safety area by drawing concentric circles with landscape paint using a string and pole for guidance.

10 ft. radius

Remove a 4"-deep layer of sod and dirt in the firepit and safety areas (the depth of the excavation depends on what materials you're installing in the safety zone.)

Dig a 4"-deep trench for the perimeter stones that will ring the pit liner.

Fill the trench for the perimeter stones with compactable gravel and tamp thoroughly. Then scatter gravel to within 2½" of the paver edging top throughout the project area. It is not necessary to tamp this layer at this time.

Place your metal fire ring so it is level on the gravel layer and centered around the center pipe.

Arrange the first course of wall blocks around the fire ring. Keep gaps even and check with a level, adding or removing gravel as needed.

Install the second course of retaining wall block, taking care to evenly stagger the vertical joints on the first and second courses. Add the remaining courses.

Compact the compactable gravel in the seating/safety area using a rental plate vibrator.

Place and compact a layer of top-dressing rock in the seating/safety area to complete the firepit.

Carpentry Projects

The structural features you'll build in this chapter provide the framework for your outdoor living space. Fences promote privacy and keep critters out, and an attractive garden shed will provide a place for you to store tools, materials, plants, and equipment. A cedar compost bin proves that a vessel for decaying vegetable matter doesn't have to be ugly.

These are all practical projects using wood. Meanwhile, we give you some beauties that will take your landscape a step above the rest: a sophisticated garden bridge and cozy arbor retreat.

In this chapter:

- Gallery
- Compost Bin
- Classic Garden Bridge
- Trellis
- Bamboo Fence
- Picket Protection Fence
- Arbor Retreat
- Remote Tool Shed

Gallery

Lath trellis is a handy wall for creating visual and wind screens, as well as for hanging container plants.

An arbor and gate serves as a formal entrance to a backyard cottage garden. The arbor is highly hospitable to climbing plants.

A low, wooden bridge spans this creekbed with great elegance.

Hanging plants from this overhead arbor tie the deck visually to the rest of the backyard landscape.

Bamboo poles are lashed together to create a fence that creates an unusual, surprising landscape effect. Bamboo is available in preformed panels, or can be assembled by joining together random pieces, as shown here.

A cedar arbor can be left unstained or you can paint it to either complement or contrast with other colors in the landscape. Either way, it makes a romantic addition to your yard while helping to direct the traffic flow.

Any shed provides extra storage for gardening tools and lawn equipment. A well-designed shed also becomes an architectural accent piece for the landscape.

An overhead arbor can be a quiet, secluded getaway spot. Or, it can be built front-and-center in your yard to become a focal point.

Even the simplest gates have a welcoming effect when they are built carefully and are well maintained.

Compost Bin

The byproducts of routine yard maintenance can pile up. Consider the waste generated by your landscaping during a single year: grass clippings, deadheaded blossoms, leaves, branches, and weeds. All this can be recycled into compost and incorporated back into plant beds as a nutrient-rich soil amendment.

Compost is nature's own mulch, and it effectively increases soil porosity, improves fertility, and stimulates healthy root development. Besides, making your own mulch or soil amendment through composting is much less expensive than buying commercial materials. Kitchen waste and yard refuse are all the ingredients you need.

So how does garbage turn into plant food? The process works like this: Organisms such as bacteria, fungi, worms, and insects convert compost materials into humus, a loamy, nutrient-rich soil. Humus is the end goal of composting, and it can take as long as a couple of years or as short as a month to produce.

With the right conditions, you can speed up Mother Nature's course and yield several helpings of fresh compost for your yard each season. This is called managed composting, as opposed to passive composting, when you allow a pile of plant debris and such to decompose on its own. The conditions must be just right to manage compost and speed the process. You'll need a balance of carbon and nitrogen, the right temperature, good air circulation, and the right amount of water. By mixing, chopping materials, and monitoring conditions in your compost pile, you'll increase your yield each season.

Tools & Materials ▸

(8) Cedar 2 × 4
(10) Cedar 1 × 2
(3 × 12 ft.) Galvanized hardware cloth (½")
Deck screws (3")

U-nails (or narrow crown staples)
(2) 2 × 2" galvanized butt hinges
Exterior wood glue

Caulk
Circular saw
Table saw (optional)
Power miter saw
Clamps

Drill/driver
Hammer
Pneumatic stapler (optional)
Caulk gun

Browns and Greens ▸

A fast-burning compost pile requires a healthy balance of "browns" and "greens." Browns are high in carbon, which is food energy microorganisms depend on to decompose the pile. Greens are high in nitrogen, which is a protein source for the multiplying microbes. A ratio of 3-to-1 brown-to-green materials is the best balance.

- Browns: Dry brown plant material, straw, dried brown weeds, wood chips, saw dust (used with caution)
- Greens: Grass clippings, kitchen fruit and vegetable scraps, green leaves, and manure

Note: If you use chemical lawn care products on your lawn, do not include grass clippings in your compost pile.

Cutting List

KEY	PART	NO.	DIM.	MATERIAL
A	Post	8	1½ × 1¾ × 48"	Cedar
B	Door rail	2	1½ × 3½ × 16"	"
C	Door rail	2	1½ × 1¾ × 16"	"
D	Door stile	4	1½ × 1¾ × 30½"	"
E	Panel rail	3	1½ × 3½ × 32½"	"
F	Panel rail	3	1½ × 1¾ × 32½"	"
G	Panel stile	3	1½ × 3½ × 30½"	"
H	Infill	16	¾ × 1½ × 30½"	"
I	Filler	80	¾ × 1½ × 4"	"
J	Panel grid frame-h	12	¾ × 1½" × Cut to fit	"

KEY	PART	NO.	DIM.	MATERIAL
K	Grid frame-v	16	¾ × 1½" × Cut to fit	Cedar
L	Door frame-h	4	¾ × 1½" × Cut to fit	"
M	Top rail-side	2	1½ × 1¾ × 39"	"
N	Top rail-back	1	1½ × 1¾ × 32½"	"
O	Front spreader	1	1½ × 3½ × 32½"	"

Also need:
½" galvanized hardware cloth 36" by 12 ft.
U-nails (fence staples)
2 pairs 2 × 2" butt hinges
3" deck screws
Exterior wood glue

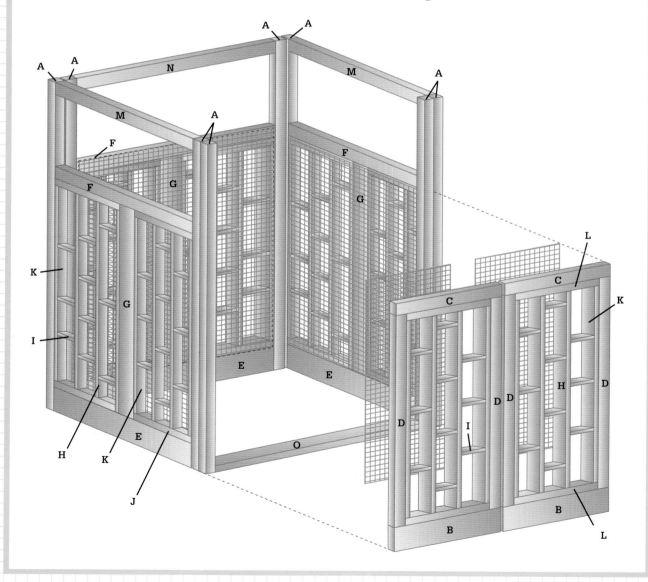

How to Build a Compost Bin

Prepare the wood stock. At most building centers and lumber yards you can buy cedar sanded on all four sides, or with one face left rough. The dimensions in this project are sanded on all four sides. Prepare the wood by ripping some of the stock into 1¾" wide strips (do this by ripping 2 × 4s down the middle on a tablesaw or with a circular saw and cutting guide).

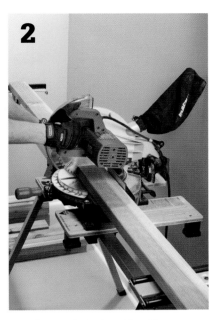

Cut the parts to length with a power miter saw or a circular saw. For uniform results, set up a stop block and cut all similar parts at once.

Assemble the door frames. Apply exterior-rated wood glue to the mating parts and clamp them together with pipe or bar clamps. Reinforce the joints with 3" countersunk deck screws (two per joint). Reinforce the bottom joints by drilling a pair of ¾"-dia. × 1" deep clearance holes up through the bottom edges of the bottom rails and driving 3" deck screws through pilot holes up into the stiles.

Assemble the side and back panels. Clamp and glue the posts and rails for each frame, making sure the joints are square. Then, reinforce the joints with countersunk 3" deck screws—at least two per joint.

(continued)

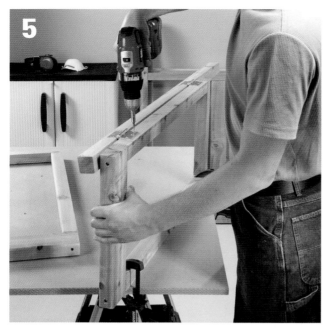

Hang the door frames. With the posts cut to length and oriented correctly, attach a door frame to each post with a pair of galvanized butt hinges. The bottoms of the door frames should be flush with or slightly higher than the bottoms of the posts. Temporarily tack a 1 × 4 brace across both door bottom rails to keep the doors from swinging during construction.

Join the panels and the door assembly by gluing and clamping the parts together and then driving 3" countersunk deck screws to reinforce the joints. To stabilize the assembly, fasten the 2 × 4 front spreader between the front, bottom edges of the side panels. Make sure the spreader will not interfere with door operation.

Make the grids for the panel infill areas. Use 1 × 2 cedar to make all parts (you may have to rip-cut cedar 2 × 4s for this, depending on availability in your area. Use exterior glue and 18-gauge brads (galvanized) to connect the horizontal filler strips to the vertical infill pieces. Vary the heights and spacing of the filler for visual interest and to make the ends accessible for nailing.

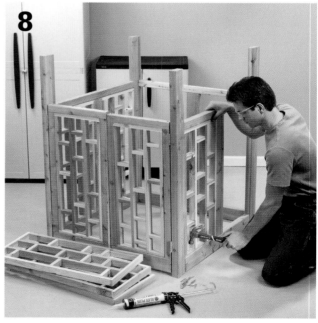

Frame the grids with 1 × 2 strips cut to the correct length so each frame fits neatly inside a panel or door opening. Install the grid frames in the openings, making sure all front edges are flush.

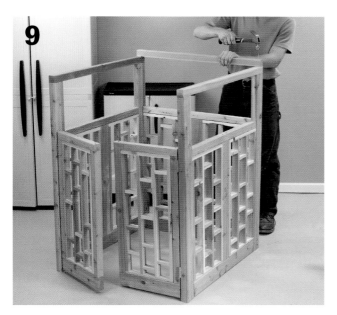

Attach the top rails that conceal the post tops and help tie the panels together. Attach the sides first using exterior glue and galvanized finish nails. Then, install the back rail on top of the side rails. Leave the front of the project open on top so you can load, unload, and turn over compost more easily.

Line the interior surfaces of the compost bin with ½" galvanized hardware cloth. Cut the hardware cloth to fit and fasten it with fence staple or galvanized U-nails driven every 6" or so. Make sure you don't leave any sharp edges protruding. Grind them down with a rotary tool or a file.

Set up the bin in your location.
Apply a coat of exterior wood sealant to all wood surfaces—use a product that contains a UV inhibitor. *Tip: Before setting up your compost bin, dig a 12"-deep hole just inside the area where the bin will be placed. This will expand your bin's capacity.*

Classic Garden Bridge

An elegant garden bridge invites you into a landscape by suggesting you stop and spend some time there. Cross a peaceful pond, traverse an arroyo of striking natural stone, or move from one garden space to the next and explore. While a bridge is practical and functions as a way to get from point A to point B, it does so much more. It adds dimension, a sense of romanticism, and the feeling of escaping to somewhere special.

The bridge you see here can be supported with handrails and trellis panels, but left simple as pictured, its Zen appeal complements projects in this book, including: arroyo, garden pond, and rain garden. We think the sleek, modern design blends well in the landscape, providing a focal point without overwhelming a space.

Tools & Materials ▸

4 × 4" × 8' cedar (4)
2 × 10" × 8' cedar (2)
2 × 4" × 8' cedar (10)
1 × 8" × 8' cedar (2)
1 × 3" × 8' cedar (2)
1 × 2" × 8' cedar (8)
½" × 2" × 8' cedar
   lattice (2)
Lag screws (⅜ × 4")
Deck screws (2", 3")

Finishing materials
Jigsaw
Circular saw
Drill

Unlike many landscape and garden bridges that are large, ornate, and designed to be the center of attention, this low cedar bridge has a certain refined elegance that is a direct result of its simple design.

Cutting List

KEY	PART	DIM.	PCS.	MATERIAL
A	Stringer	1½ × 9¼ × 96"	2	Cedar
B	Stretcher	1½ × 3½ × 27"	4	"
C	Tread	1½ × 3½ × 30"	26	"

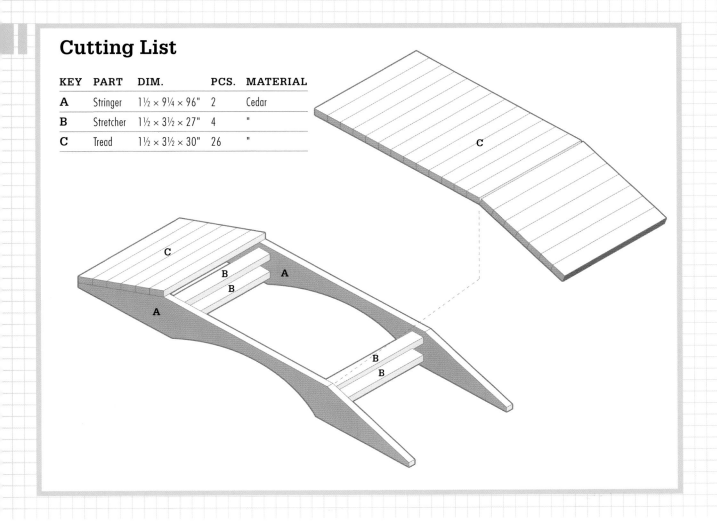

Preparing Bridge Pieces

Study the cutting list carefully and take care when measuring for cuts. The building blocks of this bridge are: stringers, a base, and treads. Read these preliminary instructions carefully, then study the steps before you begin.

Stringers: This first step involves cutting the main structural pieces of the bridge. The stringers have arcs cut into their bottom edges, and the ends of stringers are cut at a slant to create a gradual tread incline. Before you cut stringers, carefully draw guidelines on the wood pieces:

- A centerline across the width of each stringer
- Two lines across the width of each stringer 24" to the left and right of the centerline
- Lines at the ends of each stringer, 1" up from one long edge

- Diagonal lines from these points to the top of each line to the left and right of the center

Base: Four straight boards called stretchers form the base that support the bridge. Before cutting these pieces, mark stretcher locations on the insides of the stringers, 1½" from the top and bottom of the stringers. The outside edges of the stretchers should be 24" from the centers of the stringers so the inside edges are flush with the bottoms of the arcs. When working with the stretchers, the footboard may get quite heavy, so you will want to move the project to its final resting place and finish constructing the project there.

Treads: Cut the treads to size according to the cutting list. Once laid on the stringers, treads will be separated with ¼" gaps. Before you install the treads, test-fit them to be sure they are the proper size.

How to Build a Garden Bridge

Use a circular saw to cut the ends of stringers along the diagonal lines, according to the markings described on the previous page.

Tack a nail on the centerline, 5¼" up from the same long edge. Also tack nails along the bottom edge, 20½" to the left and right of the centerline.

Make a marking guide from a thin, flexible strip of scrap wood or plastic, hook it over the center nail, and slide the ends under the outside nails to form a smooth curve. Trace along the guide with a pencil to make the arc cutting line.

Use a jigsaw to make arched cut-outs in the bottoms of the 2 × 10 stringers after removing the nails and marking guide.

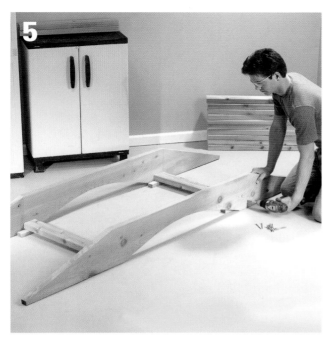

Assemble the base by preparing stringers as described on facing page and positioning the stretchers between them. Stand the stringers upright (curve at the bottom) and support bottom stretchers with 1½"-thick spacer blocks for correct spacing. Fasten stretchers between stringers with countersunk 3" deck screws, driven through the stringers and into the ends of the stretchers.

Turn the stringer assembly upside down and attach the top stretchers.

Attach treads after test-fitting them. Leave a ¼" gap between treads. Secure them with 3"-long countersunk deck screws.

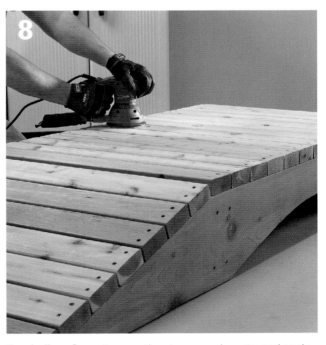

Sand all surfaces to smooth out any rough spots, and apply an exterior wood stain to protect the wood, if desired. You can leave the cedar untreated and it will turn gray, possibly blending with other landscape features.

Trellis

The primary purpose of a trellis is to support climbing plants such as clematis or morning glory. But a trellis also serves as a visually pleasing vertical design element that offers additional benefits, including blocking sun and wind. Paired with a pergola overhead structure, a trellis can provide a living screen to create an intimate nook in the landscape. Or, placed against a home or wall, a trellis adds a cottage feel to a landscape design, allowing plantlife to scale its wooden rungs and add green character to any space.

To be sure, a trellis is eye candy for a landscape. But it also must be functional, and it should accommodate the space where you want to place it and the plants it will support. So before you dig in to this project, think first: What is the purpose for this trellis? What are the growing habits of the vines that will climb the structure? Fast growers, for example, require either a taller trellis or constant pruning. Also consider what, if anything, you are trying to cover up with a trellis. Perhaps it is a utility area with garbage cans or recycling bins; maybe it is a compost area; or, it might even be an unsightly view that is not part of your property.

You can experiment with the trellis motif—how cedar pieces are arranged in patterns to form the wall. You may try diamonds, or mimic existing themes in your garden. Trellises can be polished off with a bright coat of white paint. If they are built with exterior-rated lumber or even nonwood materials, they can be left unfinished to weather naturally. Because you can buy standard trellis material in lattice form and in a few simple shapes at garden centers, strive for something a little more unique if you are building the trellis yourself. At the very least, use good sturdy stock and exterior-rated screws to create a trellis that will last for many growing seasons.

Tools & Materials ▸

Drill
Power miter saw
1 × 2 × 8 ft. cedar (10)
2 × 4 × 8 ft. cedar (1)
1¼" deck screws (ss)

½ × 4½" (3)
galvanized lag
bolts w/nuts
and washers

A well-designed trellis supports climbing plants during the growing season, and it also contributes to the appearance of the yard during the offseason when the plants die back.

Cutting List

KEY	PART	PIECES	DIMENSION
A	Base Rail	2	¾ × 1½ × 40"
B	Upright-outer	2	¾ × 1½ × 91"
C	Upright-inner	2	¾ × 1½ × 93"
D	Upright-center	1	¾ × 1½ × 89"
E	Rail	6	¾ × 1½ × 38"
F	Filler-long	2	¾ × 1½ × 24"
G	Filler-short	2	¾ × 1½ × 21"
H	Diamond	4	¾ × 1½ × 12"
I	Base	2	1½ × 3½ × 48"

(all parts cedar)

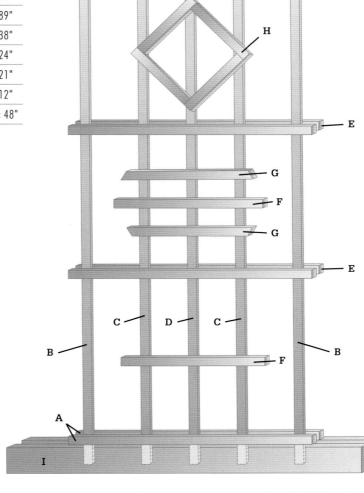

Trellis Design ▸

Sketch your trellis to scale and make a complete list of parts and sizes before you start any cutting. Choose an exterior-rated wood, such as cedar or pressure-treated pine. If you will be painting the trellis you can use dimensional construction lumber such as No. 2 or better pine. While treated lumber withstands the elements better, it is also more prone to twisting and, despite the recent switch to non-arsenic base treating chemicals, many homeowners are not comfortable working with treated lumber or using it around gardens. Choose lumber that is proportional to the scale of the project so it does not look too flimsy or clunky. Make sure, though, that the lumber is beefy enough to hold metal fasteners. For the design shown here, we used 1 × 2 cedar furring. The overall dimensions of the trellis (40 × 90") are large enough that 2 × 2 could also have been used.

How to Build a Trellis

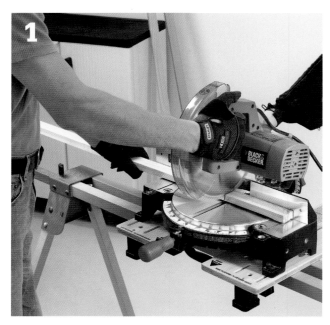

Cut the uprights and rails to length from 1 × 2 stock using a power miter saw. If your cedar stock has one rough face and one smooth, arrange the cut pieces so the faces all match.

Lay the uprights on a flat surface with their bottoms ends flush against a stop block and their edges touching. Draw reference lines across all five uprights to mark the bottom of each rail. Measuring from the bottoms, rail marks should be at the following distances: 3", 33", 57", 82½".

Spread the uprights apart with the bottoms remaining flush against the stop block. The gaps between the outer rails and the inner rail should be 8"; the gaps between the inner rails and the center rail should be 6¼". Lay rails across the uprights at the reference lines with equal overhangs at the ends. Drill a 3/32" pilot hole through each rail where it crosses each upright.

Drive a 1¼" exterior screw at each pilot hole, taking care to keep the uprights and rails in alignment. *Tip: Stainless steel screws will not rust, corrode, or cause the wood to discolor. Overdrive the screw slightly so the screwhead is recessed.*

5

Flip the assembly over once you have driven a screw at each joint on the front face. Position the second set of rails so their tops are flush with the first rails and their ends align. Drill pilot holes at each joint. Offset the pilot hole by ½" so the screws do not run into the screws driven from the other side. Drive screws to attach all four rails.

6

Attach the filler strips to the front side of the trellis according to the spacing on the diagram (page 199). Drill pilot holes so the filler strips don't split. The angled ends of the short filler strips should be cut at 30° with a power miter saw or miter box.

7

Make the decorative diamond appliqué. Cut four pieces of 1 × 2 to 12" long. Then, arrange the sticks into a diamond shape, with the end of each stick flush with the outer edge of the adjoining one. Drill a pilot hole and drive a screw at each joint. Attach the diamond shape to the top section of uprights, centered from side to side. Take care to avoid screw collisions in the diamond legs.

8

Install the base parts. The two-part 2 × 4 base seen here allows the trellis to be semi-freestanding. If it is located next to a structure you probably won't need to anchor the base to the ground, although you can use landscape spikes or pieces of rebar to anchor it if you wish. Cut the base parts to length and bolt them together, sandwiching the bottom 3" of the uprights. You can apply a UV-resistant deck finish to the wood, paint it, or let it weather.

Bamboo Fence

Bamboo is one of nature's best building materials. It's lightweight, naturally rot-resistant, and so strong that it's used for scaffolding in many parts of the world. It's also a highly sustainable resource, since many species can be harvested every three to five years without destroying the plants. Yet, perhaps the best feature of bamboo is its appearance—whether it's lined up in orderly rows or hand-tied into decorative patterns, bamboo fencing has an exotic, organic quality that adds a breath of life to any setting.

Bamboo is a grass, but it shares many properties with wood. It can be cut, drilled, and sanded with the same tools, and it takes many of the same finishes, including stains and exterior sealers. And, just like wood, bamboo is prone to splitting, though it retains much of its strength even when subject to large splits and cracks. In general, larger-diameter poles (which can be upwards of five inches) are more likely to split than smaller (such as ¾-inch-diameter) canes.

Bamboo fencing is commonly available in eight-foot-long panels made from similarly sized canes held together with internal or external wires. The panels, which are rolled up for easy transport, can be used as infill within a new wood framework, or they can attach directly to an existing wood or metal fence. Both of these popular applications are shown here. Another option is to build an all-bamboo fence using large bamboo poles for the posts and stringers and roll-up panels for the infill.

Tools & Materials ▸

Circular saw or
  reciprocating saw
Drill/driver
Countersink bit
Wire cutters
Pliers
Post hole digger
Lumber (4 × 4, 2 × 4,
  1 × 4, 2 × 6)
Deck screws
  (3", 2½", 2")
Bamboo fence panels
  with ¾"-dia. canes
Level
Tape measure
Eye and ear protection
Galvanized steel wire
Work gloves

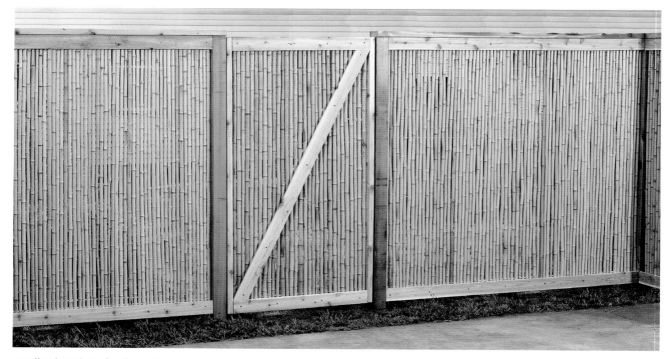

Quality bamboo for fencing isn't hard to find, but you can't pick it up at your local lumberyard. The best place to start shopping is the internet (see Resources, page 235). Look for well-established suppliers who are committed to sustainable practices. Most suppliers can ship product directly to your home.

How to Build a Wood-frame Bamboo Fence

Install and trim the 4 × 4 posts according to the size of your bamboo panels, setting the posts in concrete. For the 6 × 8-ft. panels in this project, the posts are spaced 100" on-center and are trimmed at 75" tall (refer to the manufacturer's recommendations).

Install the top 2 × 4 stringers. Cut each stringer to fit snugly between the posts. Position the stringer on edge so it is flush with the tops of the posts and with the back or front faces of the posts. Fasten the stringer with 3" deck screws driven through angled pilot holes. Use one screw on each edge and one on the inside face of the stringer, at both ends.

Mark the location of each bottom stringer. The span between the top of the top stringer and bottom of the bottom stringer should equal the bamboo panel height plus about 1". Cut and install the bottom stringers in the same fashion as the top stringers. Here, the bottom stringer will be installed 2" above the ground for rot prevention. Unroll the bamboo panels.

Flatten the bamboo panels over the inside faces of the stringers. Make sure the panels fit the frames on all sides. Using a countersink-piloting bit (inset), drill a slightly countersunk pilot hole through a bamboo cane and into the stringer at a top corner of the panel. Fasten the corner with a 2" deck screw, being careful not to overtighten and split the bamboo.

(continued)

5

Screws   2 × 4

Fasten the rest of the panel with screws spaced 12"
apart. Stagger the screws top and bottom, and drive them in
an alternating pattern, working from one side to the other.
Repeat steps 4 and 5 to install the remaining bamboo panels.

Reducing Panel Length ▶

To shorten the length of a bamboo panel,
cut the wiring holding the canes together at least two
canes beyond the desired length using wire cutters.
Remove the extra canes, and then wrap the loose
ends of wire around the last cane in the panel.

6

Cover the top and bottom ends of
the panels with 1 × 4 battens. These
finish off the panels and give the fence
a similar look on both sides. Cut the
battens so the ends are flush against the
inside faces of the posts and fasten them
to the panels and stringers with 2½"
deck screws driven through pilot holes.

7

Add the top cap. Center the 2 × 6 top cap boards over the posts so they overhang
about 1" on either side. Fasten the caps to the posts and stringers with 3" deck
screws. Use miter joints for corners, and use scarf joints (cut with opposing 30° or 45°
bevels) to join cap boards over long runs.

How to Cover an Old Fence with Bamboo

Unroll and position a bamboo panel over one or both sides of the existing fence. Check the panel with a level and adjust as needed. For rot prevention, hold the panel 1 to 2" above the ground. *Tip: A 2 × 4 laid flat on the ground makes it easy to prop up and level the panel.*

Fasten the panel with deck screws driven through the bamboo canes (and fence siding boards, if applicable) and into the fence stringers. Drill countersunk pilot holes for the screws, being careful not to overtighten and crack the bamboo. Space the screws 12" apart, and stagger them top and bottom (see facing page).

Install the remaining bamboo panels, butting the edges together between panels for a seamless appearance. If the fence posts project above the stringer boards, you can cut the bamboo panels flush with the posts.

Variation: To dress up a chain link fence with bamboo fencing, simply unroll the panels over the fence and secure them every 12" or so with short lengths of galvanized steel wire. Tie the wire around the canes or the panel wiring and over the chain link mesh.

Picket Protection Fence

Your landscape is a showpiece and testament to all the hard work and time you have invested in building, planting, and maintaining the space. But critters like deer and rabbits look at your property quite differently. To them, your landscape is a tempting, green buffet. One way to stop foragers from feasting on your landscape is to keep them out of sensitive areas—such as your garden—with fencing. That forager might be the family dog if he's prone to digging in your favorite rose bed; or the neighborhood cat that does no harm to the garden, but you'd prefer she choose another place to rest.

Meanwhile, deer are a big problem for many homeowners, especially in fast-developing communities. Their grazing habits will destroy flower beds and vegetable gardens. You'll need special fencing to protect your property from deer, and it's not always the most attractive. The best strategy is to purchase a kit, which may include a conventional 8-foot fence of woven wire. Netting will protect young shrubs and seedlings, and tubing protects tree trunks.

In this project, you'll practice basic fence-building techniques to create an attractive picket fence that will deter animals from entering your property, and contain those you want to stay within boundaries (the family dog—and yes, the kids, too). Keep in mind, fences will not deter diggers like groundhogs from invading your property. Other strategies include repellents and traps, depending on the guilty critter.

Tools & Materials ▸

For setting posts:

Plumb bob
Stakes
Hand maul
Power auger or post
   hole digger
Shovel
Coarse gravel
Carpeneter's level

Concrete
Mason's trowel
Pressure-treated
   cedar or redwood
   4 × 4 posts
Scrap lengths
   of 2 × 4

For picket fence:

Mason's string
Line level
Circular saw
Drill
Power miter saw
Sander
2-ft. level
Lumber (4 × 4,
   2 × 4, 1 × 4)
Deck screws
   (3½", 2")
Finishing materials
Hammer
Finish nails
Spacer

Speed square
Eye and ear
   protection
Clamps
Paint brush
Tape measure
16d galvanized
   common nails
Wood sealant
   or primer
Work gloves
Pencil

The shape and size of the picket tops change from fence to fence, but the classic white picket fence is a real workhorse in our landscapes and will never go out of style.

Picket Fence Styles

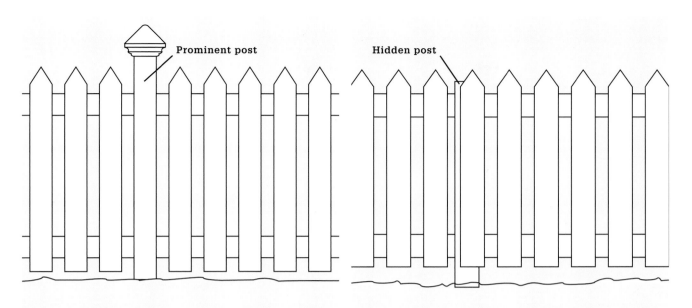

Prominent post

Hidden post

Highlighting the posts (left) gives the fence a sectional look, and the rhythm of the pickets is punctuated by the slower cadence of the posts. To create this effect, mount the stringers on edge, so the pickets are flush with—or recessed from—the front faces of the posts. Hiding the posts (right) creates an unbroken line of pickets and a somewhat less structural look overall. This effect calls for stringers installed flush with—or over the front of—the post faces.

How to Build a Picket Fence

Install and trim the posts according to your plan (see pages 30 to 33). In this project, the pickets stand at 36" above grade, and the posts are 38" (without the post caps). Set the posts in concrete, and space them as desired—but no more than 96" on center.

Mark the stringer positions onto the posts. Measure down from each post top and make marks at 8 and 28½" (or as desired for your design). These marks represent the top edges of the two stringer boards for each fence section.

(continued)

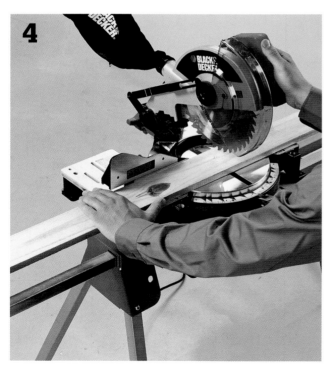

Install the stringers. Measure between each pair of posts, and cut the 2 × 4 stringers to fit. Drill angled pilot holes, and fasten the stringers to the posts with 3½" deck screws or 16d galvanized common nails; drive one fastener in the bottom and top edges of each stringer end.

Calculating Picket Spacing ▸

Determine the picket quantity and spacing. Cut a few pickets (steps 4 to 5) and experiment with different spacing to find the desired (approximate) gap between pickets. Calculate the precise gap dimension and number of pickets needed for each section using the formula shown in the example here.

Total space between posts: 92.5"
Unit size (picket width + approx. gap size):
    3.5" + 1.75" = 5.25"
Number of pickets (post space ÷ unit size):
    92.5" ÷ 5.25" = 17. 62 (round down for slightly
    larger gaps; round up for slightly smaller gaps)
Total picket area (# of pickets × picket width):
    17 × 3.5" = 59.5"
Remaining space for gaps (post space -
    total picket area): 92.5" - 59.5" = 33"
Individual gap size (total gap space ÷
    (# of pickets + 1): 33" ÷ 18 = 1.83"

Cut the pickets to length using a power miter saw. To save time, set up a stop block with the distance from the block to blade equal to the picket length. *Tip: If you're painting the fence, you can save money by cutting the pickets from 12-ft.-long boards of pressure-treated lumber. In this project, the pickets are 32" long; each board yields 4 pickets.*

Shape the picket ends as desired. For straight-cut designs, use a miter saw with a stop block on the right side of the blade (the first pass cuts through the picket and the block). If the shape is symmetrical, such as this 90° point, cut off one corner, and then flip the board over and make the second cut—no measuring or adjusting is needed.

Variation: To cut pickets with decorative custom shapes, create a cardboard or hardboard template with the desired shape. Trace the shape onto each picket and make the cuts. Use a jigsaw for curved cuts. Gang several cut pieces together for final shaping with a sander.

Prime or seal all surfaces of the posts, stringers, and pickets; and then add at least one coat of finish (paint, stain, or sealer), as desired. This will help protect even the unexposed surfaces from rot.

Set up a string line to guide the picket installation. Clamp a mason's string to two posts at the desired height for the tops of the pickets. *Note: To help prevent rot and to facilitate grass trimming, plan to install the pickets at least 2" above the ground.*

Install the pickets. Using a cleat spacer cut to the width of the picket gap, set each picket in place and drill even pairs of pilot holes into each stringer. Fasten the pickets with 2" deck screws. Check the first picket (and every few thereafter) for plumb with a level before piloting.

Add the post caps. Wood post caps (with or without metal cladding) offer an easy way to dress up plain posts while protecting the end grain from water. Install caps with galvanized or stainless steel finish nails, or as directed by the manufacturer. Apply the final finish coat or touch-ups to the entire fence.

Arbor Retreat

The airy, sun-filtered space under an arbor always makes you want to stay awhile—thus, it's a perfect place for built-in seating. The arbor getaway we've chosen (facing page) has plenty of room for lounging or visiting, but it's designed to do much more: Viewed from the front, the arbor retreat becomes an elegant passageway. The bench seating is obscured by latticework, and your eyes are drawn toward the central opening and striking horizontal beams. This makes the structure perfect as a grand garden entrance or a landscape focal point. For added seclusion, tuck this arbor behind some foliage.

Sitting inside the retreat you can enjoy privacy and shade behind the lattice screens. The side roof sections over the seats are lowered to follow a more human scale and create a cozier sense of enclosure. Each bench comfortably fits three people and the two sides face each other at a range that's ideal for conversation.

A classic archway with a keystone motif gives this arbor retreat its timeless appeal.

An arbor with benches makes an ideal resting spot that will become a destination when hiking to remote areas of your property.

A slatted roof and lattice walls are designed to cut sun and wind, creating a comfortable environment inside the arbor retreat.

A few subtle touches turn this cedar arbor into a true standout. The arches at the tops of the sidewall panels give the design visual lift and a touch of Oriental styling.

Materials List

DESCRIPTION (NO. FINISHED PIECES)	QUANTITY/SIZE	MATERIAL
Posts		
Inner posts (4)	4 @ field measure	4 × 4
Outer posts (4)	4 @ field measure	4 × 4
Concrete	Field measure	3,000 PSI concrete
Gravel	Field measure	Compactable gravel
Roof		
Beams (6 main, 4 cross)	8 @ 8'	4 × 4
Roof slats (10 lower, 11 upper)	21 @ 8'	2 × 2
Seats		
Seat supports, spacers, slats (6 horizontal supports, 6 vertical supports, 4 spacers, 16 slats)	16 @ 8'	2 × 6
Aprons (2)	2 @ 6'	1 × 8
Lattice Screens		
Arches (4)	1 @ 8'	2 × 8
Slats — arched sides (20 horizontal, 8 vertical)	12 @ 8'	2 × 2
Slats — back (8)	8 @ 8'	2 × 2
Hardware & Fasteners		
³⁄₈" × 7" galvanized lag screws	12, with washers	
3" deck screws		
3½" deck screws		
2½" deck screws		
¼" × 3" galvanized lag screws	16, with washers	

Front Elevation

Beam End Detail

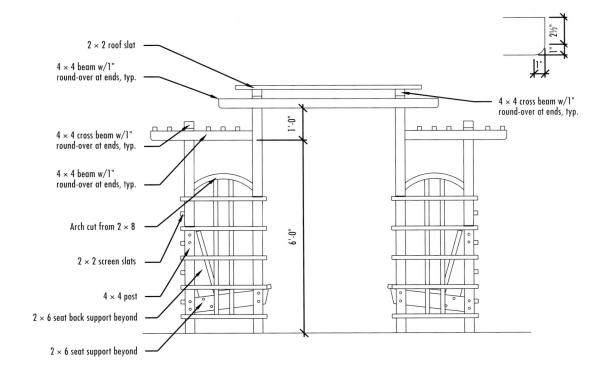

2 × 2 roof slat

4 × 4 beam w/1" round-over at ends, typ.

4 × 4 cross beam w/1" round-over at ends, typ.

4 × 4 beam w/1" round-over at ends, typ.

Arch cut from 2 × 8

2 × 2 screen slats

4 × 4 post

2 × 6 seat back support beyond

2 × 6 seat support beyond

4 × 4 cross beam w/1" round-over at ends, typ.

2½"
1"
1"

1'-0"

6'-0"

Side Elevation

Post Layout

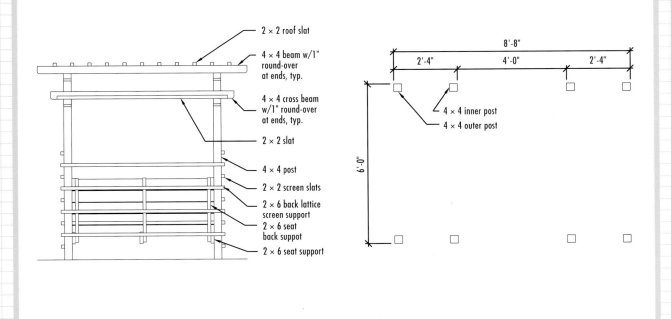

2 × 2 roof slat

4 × 4 beam w/1" round-over at ends, typ.

4 × 4 cross beam w/1" round-over at ends, typ.

2 × 2 slat

4 × 4 post

2 × 2 screen slats

2 × 6 back lattice screen support

2 × 6 seat back suppot

2 × 6 seat support

8'-8"

2'-4"   4'-0"   2'-4"

4 × 4 inner post

4 × 4 outer post

6'-0"

Upper Level Roof Framing Plan

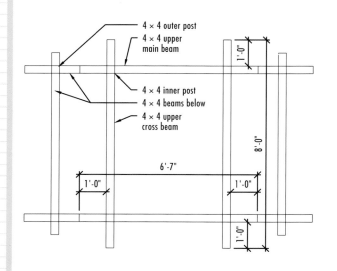

4 × 4 outer post
4 × 4 upper main beam
4 × 4 inner post
4 × 4 beams below
4 × 4 upper cross beam

1'-0"
8'-0"
6'-7"
1'-0"
1'-0"
1'-0"

Seat Framing Plan

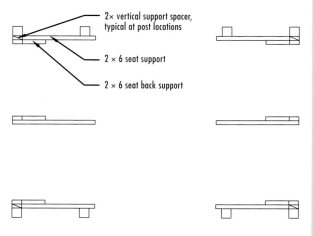

2× vertical support spacer, typical at post locations
2 × 6 seat support
2 × 6 seat back support

Roof/Slat Plan

5'-7"
6"
6"
4 × 4 beam
2 × 2 slats
8"
8"
8"
8"
8"
8"
8"
8"
8"
Centerline dimensions
4 × 4 cross beam

Slat Plan @ Seating

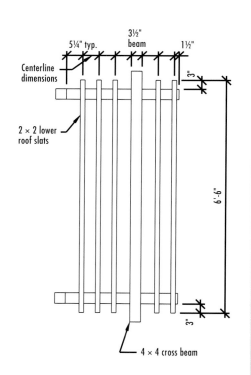

3½" beam
5¼" typ.
1½"
Centerline dimensions
3"
2 × 2 lower roof slats
6'-6"
3"
4 × 4 cross beam

Seat Section

2 × 2 roof slat
4 × 4 cross beam
4 × 4 beam
4 × 4 post

4 × 4 beam
2 × 2 slat
4 × 4 cross beam
4 × 4 post

2× vertical
support spacer
between seat back
support and post

2 × 6
back slats

2 × 6 sloped
seat back
support

2 × 6 sloped
seat support

98°

2'-6½"

2 × 6
seat slats

1" overhang
1× apron

1'-1"

6"

2'-5½"

1'-4½"

18°

Arch Detail/Screen Layout

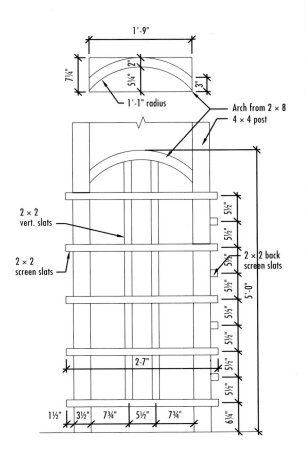

1'-9"

7¼"

2"

5¼"

3"

1'-1" radius

Arch from 2 × 8
4 × 4 post

2 × 2
vert. slats

2 × 2
screen slats

2 × 2 back
screen slats

5½"
5½"
5½"
5½"
5½"
5½"
5½"

5'-0"

2-7"

6¼"

1½"   3½"   7¾"   5½"   7¾"

Seat Level Roof Framing Plan

3'-½"

1'-0"

6"

7'-0"

4 × 4 inner post
4 × 4 lower main beam
4 × 4 outer post below
4 × 4 lower cross beam

6"

3'-½"

1'-0"

Seat Slat Layout Plan

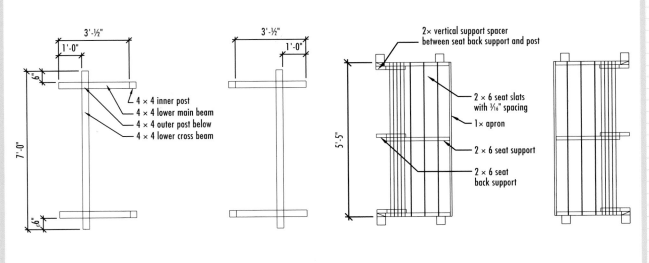

2× vertical support spacer
between seat back support and post

2 × 6 seat slats
with 3/16" spacing

1× apron

2 × 6 seat support

2 × 6 seat
back support

5'-5"

How to Build the Arbor Retreat

Stake out the project area. Drive a pair of stakes about 2 ft. outside of each corner and string mason's lines from the stakes to create a rectangle that's equal to the total project footprint (6 ft. × 8 ft. 8" as seen here). Mark post locations on the strings, as shown in the Post Layout diagram, and drive stakes at those points to mark postholes.

Set the eight posts in concrete, making sure that the tops of the four inner posts are at least 84" above the ground, and the four outer posts are 72" above ground. The size and depth of postholes should conform to local building codes. At a minimum, the postholes should be three times the diameter of the post (a 12"-dia. hole) and 24" deep. Use stakes and braces to level and plumb the posts.

Trim post tops. Let the concrete set up overnight and then mark level cutting lines on the posts tops. Use a laser level or a 4 ft. level taped to a straight 2 × 4 to transfer the cutting lines. Make sure to make all four faces of each post. Use a circular saw (a cordless trim saw is best) to trim the post tops.

Cut the lower and upper level beams. The lower level consists of four beams running perpendicular to the seats, and two beams running parallel to the seats. The upper level has two main beams and two cross beams. The 4 × 4 beams have two ends rounded over at the bottom corners with a jig saw. Cut the lower seat level beams to length at 36½". Cut the lower cross beams at 84". Cut upper level main beams to length at 79". Cut upper level cross beams at 96".

Install the lower beams. For each lower level main beam, set the beam on top of an outer post and butt its unshaped end against the corresponding inner post. Hold the beam level, and mark the point where the top face of the beam meets the inner post. Set the beam aside.

Mark a drilling point for a pilot hole on the opposite (inside) face of the inner post. Then, drill a counterbored hole just deep enough to completely recess the washer and head of a ⅜" × 7" lag screw. Reposition each beam so its top face is on the post reference line. Then drill a pilot hole for the lag screw through the inner post and into the end of the beam. Fasten each main beam with a ⅜" lag screw.

(continued)

Drill angled pilot holes through the sides of the cross beams and into the main beams, about ¾" in from the sides of the main beams (to avoid hitting the large screws). Drill two holes on each side of the cross beam at each joint. Fasten cross beams to main beams with 3½" deck screws (eight screws for each cross beam) driven toenail style.

Cut the 10 lower roof slats to length (78"). Mark the roof slat layout onto the tops of the lower main beams, following the plan on page 214. Position slats so they overhang the main beams by 3" at both ends. Drill pilot holes, and fasten the slats to the main beams with 2½" deck screws.

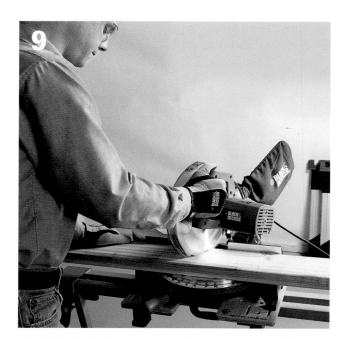

Cut seat supports according to the chart on page 215. Save the cutoffs to make seat slats. Also cut a pair of vertical support spacers from a full 2 × 6. Test-fit the pieces onto the arbor posts and make necessary adjustments. Make 18°-plumb cuts at the fronts of the seat supports.

Position the horizontal seat supports by first measuring up from the ground and marking the inner posts at 16½" and the outer posts at 13". (This marks the top edges of the horizontal supports.) Next, position the seat supports on the marks so their back ends are flush with the outsides of the outer posts. Fasten the supports to the posts with ¼" × 3" lag screws driven through counterbored pilot holes.

Position the vertical seat back support spacers and mark the locations of the support spacer onto the post. Fasten spacers to the post with 3" deck screws driven through pilot holes. Then, fasten the vertical seat back support to the spacer and horizontal seat support with 3½" deck screws; use three or four screws at each end.

Measure and cut 1 × 8 aprons to lengths so they will fit between the outside faces of the side seat supports. Bevel-cut the top edges of the aprons at 7°. Position the aprons against the seat supports. Fasten aprons to the ends of seat supports with 3½" deck screws.

Install seat slats and center supports by first measuring between inner posts for seat slat length; then cutting eight slats for each side. Position a slat on top of the horizontal seat supports so the front edge overhangs the supports by about 1". Fasten the slat to supports with pairs of 3" deck screws. Continue installing slats, leaving a ³⁄₁₆" gap between each.

Assemble the two center seat supports so they match the outer supports, using 2½" deck screws. Install the center supports at the midpoints of the slats by screwing through the slats and into the supports, using 3" deck screws.

(continued)

Build arched lattice screens by first marking the layout of horizontal lattice pieces onto the posts. Mark along one post and use a level to transfer the marks to the other post. Then cut 20 2 × 2 lattice slats to 31". Position them so they overhang the posts by 1½" at both ends and fasten slats to posts with 2½" deck screws driven through pilot holes.

Make the arches using a cardboard template to trace the shape onto a 2 × 8. Cut out the arch with a jigsaw or bandsaw and test-fit the arch between the post pairs. Make necessary adjustments and cut the remaining arches. Sand the cut edges smooth.

Fasten the arches to the posts using 2½" deck screws. First, position arches so they are flush with the outside faces of the posts and, at each end, drill an angled pilot hole upward through the bottom of the arch and into the post.

Cut eight vertical slats to a rough length of 54" (first, mark slats 7" from each post to represent the outside edges of the vertical lattice slats). Mark the top ends of the slats to match the arches by holding each slat on its reference marks. Cut the curved ends and test-fit the slats. Hold each slat in place against the arch (mark bottom for length), then cut them to length.

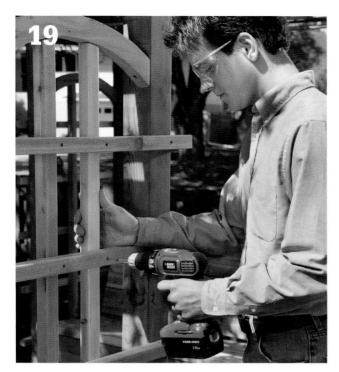

Install vertical slats with 3" deck screws driven down through tops of the arches and 2½" deck screws driven through the lowest horizontal slats. Make sure all screwheads are countersunk.

Build the back lattice screens by cutting 2 × 2 slats to length at 75", for a 1½" overhang at each end. Position the slats on layout marks, drill pilot holes, and fasten the slats to the posts with 2½" deck screws.

Finish the structure. Sand any rough areas with a random-orbit sander. Wipe down the project, and then apply a coat of exterior wood sealant/protectant.

Remote Tool Shed

The lean-to is a classic outbuilding intended as a supplementary structure for a larger building. Its simple shed-style roof helps it blend with the neighboring structure. It also directs water away and keeps leaves and debris from getting trapped between the two buildings. When built to a small shed scale, the lean-to (sometimes called a closet shed) is most useful as an easy-access storage locker that saves you extra trips into the garage for often-used lawn and garden tools and supplies.

This lean-to tool shed is designed as a freestanding building with a wooden skid foundation that makes it easy to move. With all four sides finished, the shed can be placed anywhere, but it works best when set next to a house, garage wall, or a tall fence. If you locate the shed out in the open—where it won't be protected against wind and extreme weather—be sure to anchor it securely to the ground to prevent it from blowing over.

As shown here, the shed is finished with asphalt shingle roofing, T1-11 plywood siding, and 1× cedar trim, but you can substitute any type of finish to match or complement a neighboring structure. Its 65-inch-tall double doors provide easy access to its 18 square feet of floor space. The eight-foot-tall rear wall can accommodate a set of shelves while leaving enough room below for long-handled tools.

Because the tool shed sits on the ground, in cold climates it will be subject to shifting with seasonal freeze-thaw cycles. Therefore, do not attach the tool shed to your house or any other building set on a frost-proof foundation.

A plain shed roof is about the easiest way to top a shed. This lean-to type shed is perfectly at home as a standalone shed in a remote corner of your backyard landscape (left). Or, build it right next to your house or garage (below).

Cutting List

DESCRIPTION	QUANTITY/SIZE	MATERIAL
Foundation		
Drainage material	0.5 cu. yd.	Compactable gravel
Skids	2 @ 6'	4 × 4 treated timbers
Floor framing		
Rim joists*	2 @ 6'	2 × 6 pressure-treated
Joists	3 @ 8'	2 × 6 pressure-treated
Floor sheathing	1 sheet @ 4 × 8	¾" tongue-&-groove ext.-grade plywood
Joist clip angles	4	3 × 3 × 3" × 16-gauge galvanized
Wall Framing		
Bottom plates	1 @ 8', 2 @ 6'	2 × 4
Top plates	1 @ 8', 3 @ 6'	2 × 4
Studs	14 @ 8', 8 @ 6'	2 × 4
Header	2 @ 6'	2 × 6
Header spacer	1 piece @ 6'	½" plywood — 5" wide
Roof Framing		
Rafters	6 @ 6'	2 × 6
Ledger	1 @ 6'	2 × 6
Roofing		
Roof sheathing	2 sheets @ 4 × 8'	½" ext.-grade plywood
Shingles	30 sq. ft.	250# per square min.
Roofing starter strip	7 linear ft.	
15# building paper	30 sq. ft.	
Metal drip edge	24 linear ft.	Galvanized metal
Roofing cement	1 tube	
Exterior Finishes		
Plywood siding	4 sheets @ 4 × 8'	⅝" texture 1-11 plywood siding, grooves 8" O.C.
Door trim	2 @ 8'	1 × 10 S4S cedar
	2 @ 6'	1 × 8 S4S cedar

DESCRIPTION	QUANTITY/SIZE	MATERIAL
Corner trim	6 @ 8'	1 × 4 S4S cedar
Fascia	3 @ 6'	1 × 8 S4S cedar
	1 @ 6'	1 × 4 S4S cedar
Bug screen	8" × 6'	Fiberglass
Doors		
Frame	3 @ 6'	¾" × 3½" (actual) cedar
Stops	3 @ 6'	1 × 2 S4S cedar
Panel material	12 @ 6'	1 × 6 T&G V-joint S4S cedar
Z-braces	2 @ 10'	1 × 6 S4S cedar
Construction adhesive	1 tube	
Interior trim (optional)	3 @ 6'	1 × 3 S4S cedar
Strap hinges	6, with screws	
Fasteners		
16d galvanized common nails	3½ lbs.	
16d common nails	3½ lbs.	
10d common nails	12 nails	
10d galvanized casing nails	20 nails	
8d galvanized box nails	½ lb.	
8d galvanized finish nails	2 lbs.	
8d common nails	24 nails	
8d box nails	½ lb.	
1½" joist hanger nails	16 nails	
⅞" galvanized roofing nails	¼ lb.	
2½" deck screws	6 screws	
1¼" wood screws	60 screws	

Note: 6-foot material is often unavailable at local lumber stores, so buy half as much of 12-foot material.

Floor Framing Plan

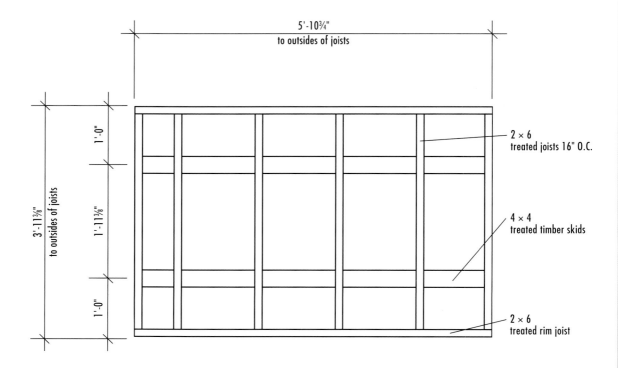

5'-10¾"
to outsides of joists

3'-11⅜"
to outsides of joists

1'-0"

1'-11⅜"

1'-0"

2 × 6
treated joists 16" O.C.

4 × 4
treated timber skids

2 × 6
treated rim joist

Roof Framing Plan

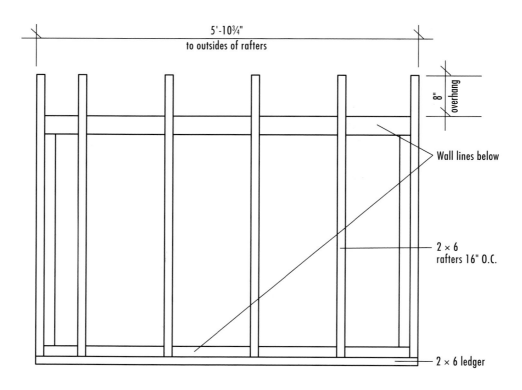

5'-10¾"
to outsides of rafters

8" overhang

Wall lines below

2 × 6
rafters 16" O.C.

2 × 6 ledger

Front Framing Elevation

2 × 6 ledger

2 × 6 rafters 16" O.C.

Double 2 × 4 top plate

2 × 4 top plate

2 - 2 × 6 header w/ ½" plywood spacer

4'-9¾" rough opening

6'-0"

5'-5" rough opening

¾" plywood

2 × 6 treated joists, 16" O.C.

4 × 4 treated timber skid

Left Framing Elevation

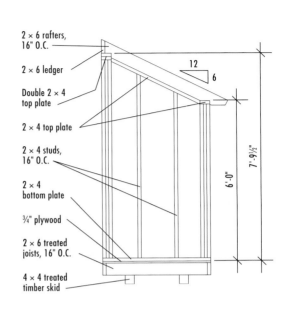

2 × 6 rafters, 16" O.C.

2 × 6 ledger

Double 2 × 4 top plate

2 × 4 top plate

2 × 4 studs, 16" O.C.

2 × 4 bottom plate

¾" plywood

2 × 6 treated joists, 16" O.C.

4 × 4 treated timber skid

12 / 6

7'-9½"

6'-0"

Rear Framing Elevation

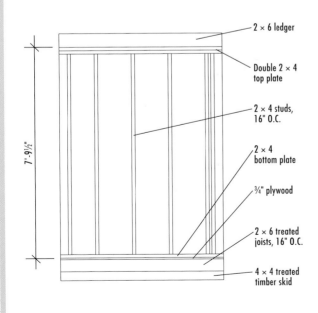

2 × 6 ledger

Double 2 × 4 top plate

2 × 4 studs, 16" O.C.

2 × 4 bottom plate

¾" plywood

2 × 6 treated joists, 16" O.C.

4 × 4 treated timber skid

7'-9½"

Right Side Framing Elevation

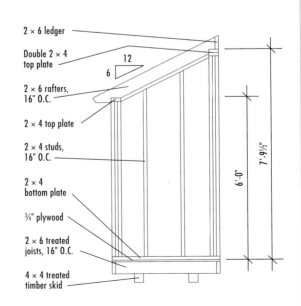

2 × 6 ledger

Double 2 × 4 top plate

2 × 6 rafters, 16" O.C.

2 × 4 top plate

2 × 4 studs, 16" O.C.

2 × 4 bottom plate

¾" plywood

2 × 6 treated joists, 16" O.C.

4 × 4 treated timber skid

12 / 6

7'-9½"

6'-0"

Building Section

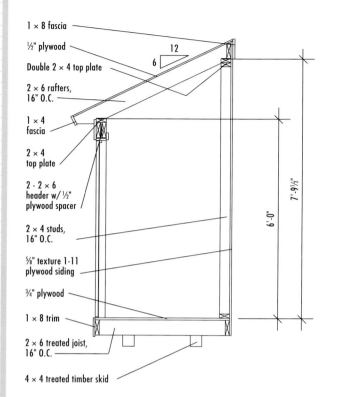

1 × 8 fascia

½" plywood

Double 2 × 4 top plate

2 × 6 rafters, 16" O.C.

1 × 4 fascia

2 × 4 top plate

2 - 2 × 6 header w/ ½" plywood spacer

2 × 4 studs, 16" O.C.

⅝" texture 1-11 plywood siding

¾" plywood

1 × 8 trim

2 × 6 treated joist, 16" O.C.

4 × 4 treated timber skid

12
6

7'-9½"

6'-0"

Side Elevation

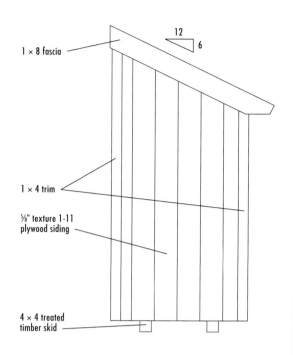

1 × 8 fascia

12
6

1 × 4 trim

⅝" texture 1-11 plywood siding

4 × 4 treated timber skid

Front Elevation

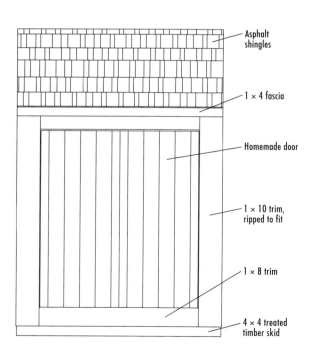

Asphalt shingles

1 × 4 fascia

Homemade door

1 × 10 trim, ripped to fit

1 × 8 trim

4 × 4 treated timber skid

Rear Elevation

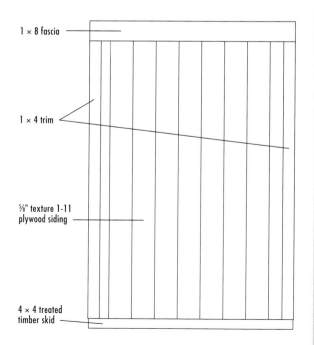

1 × 8 fascia

1 × 4 trim

⅝" texture 1-11 plywood siding

4 × 4 treated timber skid

Floor Plan

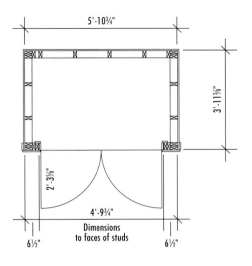

5'-10¾"

3'-11⅜"

2'-3⅜"

4'-9¾"

Dimensions
to faces of studs

6½"   6½"

Rafter Template

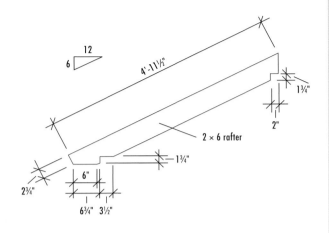

12
6

4'-11½"

1¾"

2"

2 × 6 rafter

1¾"

2¾"

6"

6¾" 3½"

Side Roof Edge Detail

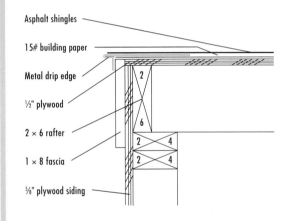

Asphalt shingles

15# building paper

Metal drip edge

½" plywood

2 × 6 rafter

1 × 8 fascia

⅝" plywood siding

Overhang Detail

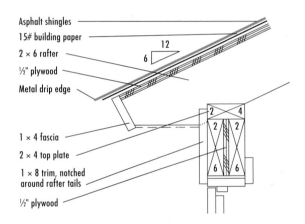

Asphalt shingles

15# building paper

2 × 6 rafter

½" plywood

Metal drip edge

12
6

1 × 4 fascia

2 × 4 top plate

1 × 8 trim, notched
around rafter tails

½" plywood

Door Jamb Detail

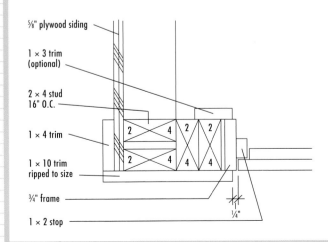

⅝" plywood siding

1 × 3 trim
(optional)

2 × 4 stud
16" O.C.

1 × 4 trim

1 × 10 trim
ripped to size

¾" frame

¼"

1 × 2 stop

Door Elevation

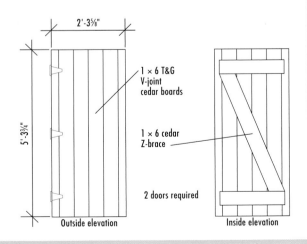

2'-3⅝"

5'-3¾"

1 × 6 T&G
V-joint
cedar boards

1 × 6 cedar
Z-brace

2 doors required

Outside elevation   Inside elevation

How to Build a Lean-to Tool Shed

Prepare the site with a 4" layer of compacted gravel. Cut the two 4 × 4 skids at 70¾". Set and level the skids following Floor Framing Plan (page 224). Cut two 2 × 6 rim joists at 70¾" and six joists at 44⅜". Assemble the floor and set it on the skids as shown in the Floor Framing Plan. Check for square, and then anchor the frame to the skids with four joist clip angles (inset photo). Sheath the floor frame with ¾" plywood.

Cut plates and studs for the walls: Side walls—two bottom plates at 47⅞", four studs at 89", and four studs at 69"; Front wall—one bottom plate at 63¾", one top plate at 70¾", and four jacks studs at 63½". Rear wall—one bottom plate at 63¾", two top plates at 70¾", and six studs at 89". Mark the stud layouts onto the plates.

Fasten the four end studs of each side wall to the bottom plate. Install these assemblies. Construct the built-up 2 × 6 door header at 63¾". Frame and install the front and rear walls, leaving the top plates off at this time. Nail together the corner studs, making sure they are plumb. Install the rear top plates flush to the outsides of the side wall studs. Install the front top plate in the same fashion.

Cut the six 2 × 6 rafters following the Rafter Template (page 227). Cut the 2 × 6 ledger at 70¾" and bevel the top edge at 26.5° so the overall width is 4⁵⁄₁₆". Mark the rafter layout onto the wall plates and ledger, as shown in the Roof Framing Plan (page 224), then install the ledger flush with the back side of the rear wall. Install the rafters.

Complete the side wall framing. Cut a top plate for each side to fit between the front and rear walls, mitering the ends at 26.5°. Install the plates flush with the outsides of the end rafters. Mark the stud layouts onto the side wall bottom plates, then use a plumb bob to transfer the marks to the top plate. Cut the two studs in each wall to fit, mitering the top ends at 26.5°. Install the studs.

Sheath the side walls and rear walls with plywood siding, keeping the bottom edges ½" below the floor frame and the top edges flush with the tops of the rafters. Overlap the siding at the rear corners, and stop it flush with the face of the front wall.

Add the 1 × 4 fascia over the bottom rafter ends as shown in the Overhang Detail (page 227). Install 1 × 8 fascia over the top rafter ends. Position all fascia ½" above the rafters so it will be flush with the roof deck. Overhang the front and rear fascia to cover the ends of the side fascia, or plan to miter all fascia joints. Cut the 1 × 8 side fascia to length, and then clip the bottom front corners to meet the front fascia. Install the side fascia.

Install the ½" roof sheathing, starting with a full-width sheet at the bottom edge of the roof. Fasten metal drip edge along the front edge of the roof. Cover the roof with building paper, then add the drip edge along the sides and top of the roof. Shingle the roof and finish the top edge with cut shingles or a solid starter strip.

(continued)

9

Cut and remove the bottom plate inside the door opening. Cut the 1 × 4 head jamb for the door frame at 57⅛" and cut the side jambs at 64". Fasten the head jamb over the sides with 2½" deck screws. Install 1 × 2 doorstops ¾" from the front edges of jambs, as shown in the Door Jamb Detail (page 227). Install the frame in the door opening using shims and 10d casing nails.

10

For each door, cut six 1 × 6 tongue-and-groove boards at 63¾". Fit them together, then mark and trim the two end boards so the total width is 27⅝". Cut the 1 × 6 Z-brace boards following the Door Elevation (page 227). The ends of the horizontal braces should be 1" from the door edges. Attach the braces with construction adhesive and 1¼" screws. Install each door with three hinges.

11

Staple fiberglass insect screen along the underside of the roof, securing it to each rafter. Cut and install the 1 × 8 trim above the door, overlapping the side door jambs about ¼" on each side (see the Overhang Detail, page 227).

12

Rip vertical and horizontal trim boards to width. Notch the ripped 1 × 8 to fit around the rafters, as shown in the Door Overhang Detail (page 227). Notch the top ends of the ripped 1 × 10s to fit between the rafters and install them. Add the notched 1 × 8 trim horizontally below the door, between the 1 × 10s. Install the 1 × 4 corner trim, overlapping the pieces at the rear corners.

APPENDIX: Codes & Considerations

For almost any building project, there are local regulations you should consider. Building codes, zoning ordinances, and permits are the legal issues you'll have to contend with, but you should also consider how your project will fit into the neighborhood and the effect it will have on your neighbors.

Building codes exist to ensure that the materials and construction methods of your project are safe. Zoning laws govern the size, location, and style of your structure to preserve aesthetic standards. Permits and inspections are required to ensure your plans meet all local building and zoning restrictions.

Requirements and restrictions vary from one community to the next, so make sure to check the codes for your area. If your plans conflict with local codes, you may be able to apply for a variance, which allows you to bypass the strict requirements of the code. In some cases, you'll need the agreement of your neighbors in order to obtain a variance.

Talk to your local building inspection department early to determine if your project requires a permit and whether you must submit plans for approval. The permit process can take several weeks or months, so checking early helps avoid delays. Fill out the necessary forms, pay any applicable fees, and wait for your approval.

Discuss your plans with neighbors as well. A fence, wall, or gate on or near a property line is as much a part of your neighbors' landscapes as your own. The tall hedge you've planned for privacy may cast a dense shadow over your neighbor's sunbathing deck. The simple courtesy of letting your neighbors know what you're planning can keep everyone on a friendly basis, and can even help avoid legal disputes.

You may find that discussing your plans with neighbors reaps unexpected rewards. You and your neighbor may decide to share labor and expenses by landscaping both properties at once. Or you may combine resources on a key feature that benefits both yards, such as a stone garden wall or shade tree.

In addition, check with your local utility companies to pinpoint the locations of any underground electrical, plumbing, sewer, or telephone lines on your property. These locations can have an impact on your plans if your project requires digging or changes your property's grade. There is no charge to have utility companies locate these lines, and it can prevent you from making an expensive or life-threatening mistake. In many areas, the law requires that you have this done before digging any holes.

On the following pages, you'll find some common legal restrictions for typical landscape projects.

FENCES

- **Height:** The maximum height of a fence may be restricted by your local building code. In some communities, backyard fences are limited to 6 ft. in height, while front yard fences are limited to 3 ft. or 4 ft.—or prohibited altogether.
- **Setback:** Even if not specified by your building code, it's a good idea to position your fence 12" or so inside the official property line to avoid any possible boundary disputes. Correspondingly, don't assume that a neighbor's fence marks the exact boundary of your property. For example, before digging an elaborate planting bed up to the edge of your neighbor's fence, it's best to make sure you're not encroaching on someone else's land.
- **Gates:** Gates must be at least 3 ft. wide. If you plan to push a wheelbarrow through it, your gate width should be 4 ft.

DRIVEWAYS

- **Width:** Straight driveways should be at least 10 ft. wide; 12 ft. is better. On sharp curves, the driveway should be 14 ft. wide.
- **Thickness:** Concrete driveways should be at least 6" thick.
- **Base:** Because it must tolerate considerable weight, a concrete or brick paver driveway should have a compactible gravel base that is at least 6" thick.
- **Drainage:** A driveway should slope ¼" per foot away from a house or garage. The center of the driveway should be crowned so it is 1" higher in the center than on the sides.
- **Reinforcement:** Your local building code probably requires that all concrete driveways be reinforced with iron rebar or steel mesh for strength.

SIDEWALKS & PATHS

- **Size of sidewalks:** Traditional concrete sidewalks should be 4 ft. to 5 ft. wide to allow two people to comfortably pass one another, and 3" to 4" thick.
- **Width of garden paths:** Informal pathways may be 2 ft. to 3 ft. wide, although stepping-stone pathways can be even narrower.
- **Base:** Most building codes require that a concrete or brick sidewalk be laid on a base of compactible gravel at least 4" thick. Standard concrete sidewalks may also need to be reinforced with iron rebar or steel mesh for strength.

- **Surface & drainage:** Concrete sidewalk surfaces should be textured to provide a nonslip surface, and crowned or slanted ¼" per foot to ensure that water doesn't puddle.
- **Sand-set paver walkways:** Brick pavers should be laid on a 3"-thick base of sand.

Fences should be set back at least 1 ft. from the formal property lines.

Driveways should be at least 10 ft. wide to accommodate vehicles.

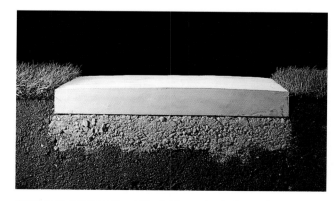

Concrete paving should be laid on a bed of gravel to provide drainage.

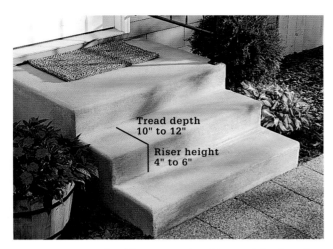

Concrete steps should use a comfortable tread depth and riser height.

Concrete patios require reinforcement with steel mesh or rebar.

Mortared garden walls need to be supported by concrete footings.

STEPS

- **Proportion of riser to tread depth:** In general, steps should be proportioned so that the sum of the depth, plus the riser multiplied by two, is between 25" and 27". A 15" depth and 6" rise, for example, is a comfortable step (15 + 12 = 27); as is an 18" depth and 4" rise (18 + 8 = 26).
- **Railings:** Building codes may require railings for any stairway with more than three steps, especially for stairs that lead to an entrance to your home.

CONCRETE PATIOS

- **Base:** Concrete patios should have a subbase of compactible gravel at least 4" thick. Concrete slabs for patios should be at least 3" thick.
- **Reinforcement:** Concrete slabs should be reinforced with wire mesh or a grid of rebar.

GARDEN WALLS

- **Footings:** Mortared brick or stone garden walls more than 4 ft. in height often require concrete footings that extend below the winter frost line. Failure to follow this regulation can result in a hefty fine or a demolition order, as well as a flimsy, dangerous wall.
- **Drainage:** Dry-set stone garden walls installed without concrete footings should have a base of compactible gravel at least 4" thick to ensure the stability of the wall.

SWIMMING POOLS

- **Fences:** Nearly all building codes require a protective fence around swimming pools to keep young children and animals away from the water.
- **Location:** In some areas, building codes require that below-ground swimming pools be at least 10 ft. away from a building foundation.

RETAINING WALLS

- **Height:** For do-it-yourself construction, retaining walls should be no more than 4 ft. high. Higher slopes should be terraced with two or more short retaining walls.
- **Batter:** A retaining wall should have a backward slant (batter) of 2" to 3" for dry-set stones; 1" to 2" for mortared stones.
- **Footings:** Retaining walls higher than 4 ft. must have concrete footings that extend down below the frost line. This helps ensure the stability of the wall.

PONDS

- **Safety:** To ensure child safety, some communities restrict landscape ponds to a depth of 12" to 18", unless surrounded by a protective fence or covered with heavy wire mesh.

DECKS

- **Structural members:** Determining the proper spacing and size for structural elements of a deck can be a complicated process, but if you follow these guidelines, you will satisfy code requirements in most areas:

A series of short retaining walls, rather than one tall wall, is the best way to handle a slope.

BEAM SIZE & SPAN	
Beam size	**Maximum spacing between posts**
two 2 × 8s	8 ft.
two 2 × 10s	10 ft.
two 2 × 12s	12 ft.
JOIST SIZE & SPAN	
Joist size	**Maximum distance between beams (Joists 16" apart)**
2 × 6	8 ft.
2 × 8	10 ft.
2 × 10	13 ft.

Railing balusters are required by building code to be spaced no more than 4" apart to keep small children from slipping through or being trapped between them.

- **Decking boards:** Surface decking boards should be spaced so the gaps between boards are no more than ¼" wide.
- **Railings:** Any deck more than 24" high requires a railing. Gaps between rails or balusters should be no more than 4".
- **Post footings:** Concrete footings should be at least 8" in diameter. If a deck is attached to a permanent structure, the footings must extend below the frost line in your region.

SHEDS

- **Setback:** Most zoning laws require that outbuildings must be set back a specific distance from property lines. Depending on your community, the distance could be as little as 6" or as much as 3 ft. or more.
- **Building permits:** These are often required if the shed has wiring and plumbing or if it exceeds a maximum size defined as a temporary structure.

Sheds larger than 120 sq. ft. may require a permit, but temporary structures typically do not.

Conversions

Metric Equivalent

Inches (in.)	1/64	1/32	1/25	1/16	1/8	1/4	3/8	2/5	1/2	5/8	3/4	7/8	1	2	3	4	5	6	7	8	9	10	11	12	36	39.4
Feet (ft.)																								1	3	3 1/12
Yards (yd.)																									1	1 1/12
Millimeters (mm)	0.40	0.79	1	1.59	3.18	6.35	9.53	10	12.7	15.9	19.1	22.2	25.4	50.8	76.2	101.6	127	152	178	203	229	254	279	305	914	1,000
Centimeters (cm)							0.95	1	1.27	1.59	1.91	2.22	2.54	5.08	7.62	10.16	12.7	15.2	17.8	20.3	22.9	25.4	27.9	30.5	91.4	100
Meters (m)																								.30	.91	1.00

Converting Measurements

TO CONVERT:	TO:	MULTIPLY BY:
Inches	Millimeters	25.4
Inches	Centimeters	2.54
Feet	Meters	0.305
Yards	Meters	0.914
Miles	Kilometers	1.609
Square inches	Square centimeters	6.45
Square feet	Square meters	0.093
Square yards	Square meters	0.836
Cubic inches	Cubic centimeters	16.4
Cubic feet	Cubic meters	0.0283
Cubic yards	Cubic meters	0.765
Pints (U.S.)	Liters	0.473 (Imp. 0.568)
Quarts (U.S.)	Liters	0.946 (Imp. 1.136)
Gallons (U.S.)	Liters	3.785 (Imp. 4.546)
Ounces	Grams	28.4
Pounds	Kilograms	0.454
Tons	Metric tons	0.907

TO CONVERT:	TO:	MULTIPLY BY:
Millimeters	Inches	0.039
Centimeters	Inches	0.394
Meters	Feet	3.28
Meters	Yards	1.09
Kilometers	Miles	0.621
Square centimeters	Square inches	0.155
Square meters	Square feet	10.8
Square meters	Square yards	1.2
Cubic centimeters	Cubic inches	0.061
Cubic meters	Cubic feet	35.3
Cubic meters	Cubic yards	1.31
Liters	Pints (U.S.)	2.114 (Imp. 1.76)
Liters	Quarts (U.S.)	1.057 (Imp. 0.88)
Liters	Gallons (U.S.)	0.264 (Imp. 0.22)
Grams	Ounces	0.035
Kilograms	Pounds	2.2
Metric tons	Tons	1.1

Converting Temperatures

Convert degrees Fahrenheit (F) to degrees Celsius (C) by following this simple formula: Subtract 32 from the Fahrenheit temperature reading. Then mulitply that number by 5/9. For example, 77°F - 32 = 45. 45 × 5/9 = 25°C.

To convert degrees Celsius to degrees Fahrenheit, multiply the Celsius temperature reading by 9/5, then add 32. For example, 25°C × 9/5 = 45. 45 + 32 = 77°F.

Fahrenheit　　　　　　**Celsius**

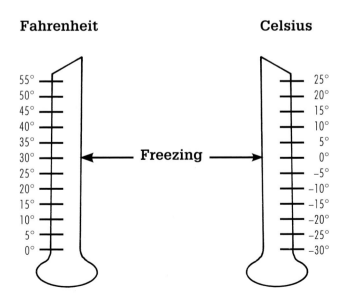

Resources/Photo Credits

Black & Decker
Portable power tools and more
www.blackanddecker.com

Cali Bamboo
Bamboo fencing, flooring, and more
888.788.2254
www.calibamboo.com

California Redwood Association
www.calredwood.com

North American One-Call Referral System
Call before you dig!
888.258.0808

Red Wing Shoes Co.
work shoes and boots shown throughout book
800 733 9464
www.redwingshoes.com

United States National Arboretum
USDA gardening zone maps
www.usna.usda.gov/Hardzone

Photo Credits

Alamy
p. 185 top

iStockphoto
pp. 11 right, 100

Mark Turner/Getty Images
p. 83 top

Photolibrary
pp. 41 bottom, 65 bottom right, 186 bottom left, 187 bottom

Photosearch
pp. 107 top, 130 bottom left, 130 top

Shutterstock
pp. 11 left, 38 both, 39 both, 40 all, 41 top, 42 top, 52, 65 bottom left, 82 both, 83 bottom, 84 all, 85 both, 92, 96-97, 106 both, 107 bottom, 108 both, 109 both, 130 bottom right, 131 all, 132 all, 133 all, 140, 184 both, 185 bottom, 186 top and bottom right, 187 top

Index

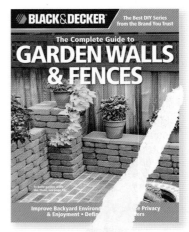

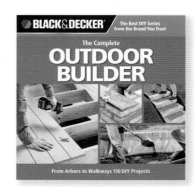